Vlasti

Sa puno justvraye

iste.

INSIGHTS
ON PERSONAL GROWTH

ADDITIONAL BOOKS BY THE AUTHOR

Insights On Policy, 2011

Insights on Management, 2011

How to Manage in Times of Crisis, 2009

The Ideal Executive: Why You Cannot Be One and What to Do About It
LEADERSHIP TRILOGY, VOL. 1, 2004

Management/Mismanagement Styles:
How to Identify a Style and What to Do About It:
LEADERSHIP TRILOGY, VOL. 2, 2004

Leading the Leaders: How to Enrich Your Style of Management
and Handle People Whose Style is Different from Yours:
LEADERSHIP TRILOGY, VOL. 3, 2004

Managing Corporate Lifecycles: An Updated and
Expanded Look at the Classic Work,
CORPORATE LIFECYCLES, 2004

The Pursuit of Prime, 1996

Mastering Change: The Power of Mutual Trust and Respect, 1992

Corporate Lifecycles: How and Why Corporations Grow and Die
and What to Do About It, 1988

How to Solve the Mismanagement Crisis, 1979

Self-Management: New Dimensions to Democracy,
with Elisabeth M. Borgese, 1975

Industrial Democracy: Yugoslav Style, 1971

To place an order or see a full list of Adizes publications,
including books and DVDs, visit us online at www.adizes.com/store.

INSIGHTS
ON
PERSONAL
GROWTH

ICHAK KALDERON ADIZES

Founder, Adizes Institute
Santa Barbara, California

Library of Congress Cataloging-in-Publication Data

Adizes, Ichak.
Insights on Personal Growth

Library of Congress Control Number Pending

ISBN: 978-0-937120-23-1

Published by
Adizes Institute Publications
1212 Mark Avenue
Carpinteria
Santa Barbara County, California, USA 93013
805-565-2901; Fax 805-565-0741
Website: www.adizes.com

Design and layout by RJ Communications LLC, New York
Printed in the United States of America

Additional copies may be ordered from www.adizes.com/store

This book is dedicated to the current living Master,
Parthasarathi Rajagopalachari
(also known as Master Chariji),
the spiritual leader of Sahaj Marg meditation

ACKNOWLEDGMENTS

I want to thank my editor, Nan Goldberg, whose editing has helped me sharpen my thinking.

CONTENTS

INTRODUCTION

THE Adizes blog, which is updated at least once a week on the Adizes Institute website and sent by e-mail to thousands of subscribers, began life in 2003 as a monthly column called "Insights."

They were, literally, *insights*, rather than the products of scientific research. I dared to say what I thought. In doing so, I opened myself up to criticism. And that is what I got: Many people wrote to say they disagreed with one or more of my observations or conclusions. But they kept reading, because what I wrote made them think. Which is exactly what I had set out to achieve.

Recently, I decided to publish the essays in book form. I cherish books; I suppose in that way I will always belong to the pre-Internet generation. The Internet, blogs, and tweets are great for speed and mass distribution, but to me they seem temporary, perishable, while a book has permanency.

In this book—the third in a series of *Insights* collections—all of the essays deal with personal growth, which I have come to believe is closely related to professional development. The ideas for these columns often evolved out of something I saw or heard or felt as I met with people around the world, observing how often their family problems echoed the organizational problems I was there to repair.

I am neither a family therapist nor a psychiatrist. Nevertheless, it has not escaped me that my theories of management and change can also be productive when applied to personal and family life. Whether the subject is meditation, divorce, or addiction (to food, to technology, or to work itself), what happens in the private realm often affects the professional realm, and vice versa. I decided to write down the insights that occurred to me about personal life.

Once these essays were published on my website (http://www.adizes. com/blog/, in light of the response from my readers, I often rethought the essays, re-edited or rewrote them, and also updated the ones that needed it. So here, in that somewhat changed form, are my thoughts as they evolved at the beginning of the 21st century, as I witnessed changes—and their unintended consequences—occurring in families all over the world.

In particular, these Insights offer a fascinating close-up of how people in developed countries, as well as countries in transition, are dealing with the phenomenon of globalization in their personal and family lives.

I hope these Insights will stir debate.

— Ichak Kalderon Adizes, Ph.D.

PART 1

SELF-KNOWLEDGE

THE MYTHS OF HAPPINESS: WHAT IS HAPPINESS, AND HOW CAN WE ACHIEVE IT?[1]

EVERYONE wants to be happy, right? Even the United States Declaration of Independence states that everyone has an inalienable right to pursue happiness. But how *do* people pursue happiness?

Would you agree that many of us equate pursuing happiness with pursuing pleasure?

That assumption, that pleasure equals happiness, is the first myth of happiness.

We pursue pleasure by maximizing sex, seeking the richest food, driving expensive cars, smoking and drinking, and, in extreme cases, by taking consciousness-changing drugs—cocaine, heroin, or marijuana.

But does pleasure bring happiness?

If you want to meet miserable people, just visit Hollywood, which is populated by people who can afford all the pleasures the world has to offer. Many of them die from drug overdoses.

So how *should* one pursue happiness?

GOOD HEALTH IS NOT SUFFICIENT

The first prerequisite is being healthy. Have you ever seen a sick person who is happy?

But herein hides the second myth of happiness: the belief that if your body is healthy, you will be happy overall.

This myth, seeking happiness in a healthy body, has caused the exercise industry to mushroom. People are jogging and stretching and puffing, but

---

[1] Adizes Insights, August 2008.

how happy are they? They are not depressed, granted, but are they happy?

Being physically healthy is a "need to" in order to be happy. It is a necessity, but not a sufficient condition alone.

To be happy overall, you also need to be emotionally happy, right? Have you ever seen a happy person who has an untreated bipolar disorder? Or a happy person with any mental disorder, for that matter?

But even being emotionally happy is not enough. Some people are addicted to seeking happiness through personal growth workshops. So emotional happiness is the third myth of happiness.

The fourth myth is that we can find happiness by avoiding the inevitable pain of having to relate to someone else, perhaps a spouse, whose style is different from ours.

But we human beings are not solitary animals. We are social animals. We congregate. The isolation of prison is a punishment. Sadhus in India isolate themselves from civilization, living in caves and meditating all day long. They might be happy, but would *you* call that a life lived to the fullest?

Thus, we need each other, but we are different. And differences cause pain. Running away from relationships is running away from one problem only to fall into another: the problem of solitude, loneliness, and a sense of failure.

Pleasure. Healthy body. Emotional happiness. Having good friends. These are all necessary conditions for being happy—but still they are not sufficient conditions for overall happiness.

THE POWER OF LOVE

What is needed to attain happiness is the integration of all of the above conditions. And that ultimate integration is *love*.

The more love in your life, the happier you will be.

Start with the entity closest to you: yourself. Do you love yourself? Are you taking care of yourself? If you do not take care of your body, where are you going to live? Do you feed your body right? Do you sleep enough? Exercise? Do you feed yourself emotionally, intellectually, and spiritually? If you do not take care of yourself, who will?

Next, do you love your spouse, your children? Extended family? Home? Car? Job? Even the books you read? The city you live in? The country you live in? Your friends? Everything you come in contact with?

The more love in your life, the happier you will be.

Love does not mean pleasure. The difference between love and pleasure is the difference between liking and loving: You like *because of.* You love *in spite of.*

It is true that the people or things you love will not always give you pleasure. On the contrary, they will give you pain, too.

Why? The more pleasure they give you, the more pain you will feel when that pleasure is missing. And it *will* be missing from time to time, because life is change. As time passes or conditions change, the things or people you love might not always be there, *as* you want them to be, *when* you want them to be.

But there is no love without pain. You will be unhappy from time to time. So love anyway, *despite* the reality that your love might periodically cause you pain.

Happiness is not a destination or a journey.

It is the condition of your journey.

The fifth myth of happiness is to expect to always be happy. But that cannot happen: Life is change. It is a roller coaster: sometimes up, sometimes down.

> The people or things you love do not always give you pleasure. On the contrary.

Someone told me once, "When you are unhappy with your spouse, just wait two days. Your feelings in two days will be different."

IT ISN'T ALL ABOUT YOU

What else is necessary?

To find happiness, you have to be spiritual. You have to be conscious of powers higher than yourself, and of absolute rules of behavior that set boundaries.

If you see yourself as the center of the world, free to do whatever you wish to do, you will find yourself more often miserable than happy. No human being has the power to control all that he wishes for.

How happy are narcissistic top executives or politicians? In spite of their achievements, my experience is that they are frustrated by their inability to control everything their egos desire.

Whenever we climb to the top of one mountain, we discover another, even higher peak to climb. Eventually, our expectations will exceed our capabilities, creating frustration and disillusionment.

Galileo proved that the sun does not move around the earth; it is the earth that orbits the sun. By analogy, we need to realize that we, human beings, circle and move around a higher consciousness that is eternal, and not vice versa. Without that anchor, we are lost in space.

We need to recognize that we are not in control; we need to yield to life's realities. Recognizing how small we are in the grand scheme of life makes us less arrogant, more humble. It frees us from being upset with ourselves when what we wish for is unattainable.

My point here is that it is OK to want, but it is not OK to expect. When we expect, we subconsciously assume that we are in control. We *should* have desires and do the best we can to get what we want, but we should not expect. We need to let be what will be.

Seek pleasure and take care of your body and your emotional health; have good friends and surround yourself with love; but at the same time, do not treat yourself and your search for happiness as the center of the world. Remember who you are and where you stand, where you come from and where you will eventually end. Like all of us.

ON EFFECTIVENESS
IN PERSONAL LIFE[1]

IN one of my Insights, I discussed what effectiveness means in managing a
business organization: A system is effective when it functions to produce
the results that fulfill the purpose for which that system was created.

It's easy to apply to a business organization: If it is a shoe company, for
instance, its purpose is to offer shoes to the market, at a price customers will
buy, so that the company will make a profit.

Now, what does it mean for a *person* to be effective in her personal life?

To answer this question, you must first ask: "What is the purpose of my
life? Why was I created?"

Hmmm.... This is not a simple question. Millions of pages have been
written on the subject, starting with religious writings and ending with
the wave of self-actualization advice that is currently engulfing modern
civilization.

Let me see if I can add to the discussion.

How can you determine whether you are effective as a human being,
whether you are producing results that fulfill the purpose of your life—that
you are not just functioning, going through the motions, producing results
but feeling that you are wasting your life?

To be effective, you have to focus first of all on why you exist. Why are
you alive?

In all the languages I know, the word "why" is nearly synonymous with
the words "what for." For instance, in Spanish: *por que* and *para que*; in
Hebrew: *lama / lema*; and in Serbian: *zasto*, which is one word meaning both
"why"—*zasto*—and "what for"—*za sto*.

I suggest that you focus on the question "What for?" That will help

---

[1] Adizes Insights, May 2008.

you determine your purpose in life much better than the question "Why?" "What for?" converges your thoughts, while the question "Why?" *di*verges your thoughts, causing you to look everywhere and nowhere for an answer.

So, instead of asking yourself *why* you exist, ask yourself, "*For what* am I here on this earth?" And you can also substitute the question "For whom?" In both cases, you are looking beyond yourself. When you serve yourself only, you are like a cancer, which uses energy for its own interests alone (assuming that death is not a purpose we aim for).

In other words, you will not discover the purpose of your life sitting in a barrel like Diogenes did, or meditating in a cave, like the Sadhus in India do. You need to go out to the market and serve someone else's needs, like Socrates did.

YOUR PERSONAL REASON FOR BEING

Now, how do you answer this question: "For whom or for what do I exist?"

Missionaries know their purpose perfectly well. Good teachers do, too. And first-class consultants, as well. (I am not so sure I can say that for lawyers. I wonder what they see as their personal mission in life. To serve whom? What? To serve "justice"? A lawyer friend of mine, when I wanted to sue someone, told me to forget it; if I want justice, he said, I should buy myself a dog and call it Justice.)

Do you know "for whom" and "for what" you exist?

Let me ask you: What inspires you? The word "inspire" (in-spire) comes from the words "to breathe into," or "God-breathed" (God breathing your soul into your body)[2]—in other words, being integrated with the biggest force there is (and you can define what that total, absolute force is for yourself)—to the point of losing yourself, forgetting time, place, everything. It is like an orgasm: For a few seconds you have no sense of time or place.

When you are inspired in your work, it feels like one prolonged mental orgasm.

Furthermore, when you are inspired in what you do, like an orgasm, your work *gives* you energy instead of *taking* energy. In contrast, when you do something you are alienated from, something you hate, it exhausts you.

---

[2] I thank Wayne Dyer for this insight.

So, what is it that uplifts you, that causes you to lose yourself in doing it—that gives you energy? And remember that it has to be serving something. If it is serving only yourself, that can also be orgasmic, but that is like masturbation: You lose energy instead of gaining it. What is it that gives you energy when you are serving others, serving something else? Whatever it is, *that* is what you should do! That is you. That is what you exist for, and if you spend your life doing it, you will not feel that you have "worked and slaved" all your life.

This is especially important as you get older and feel you have less and less energy, when you have no more children to raise and are no longer working in an organization and serving a purpose. Do not go to an old-age home and wait to die. Volunteer for something you deeply care for. Serve. You will feel younger and live longer.

> It is not the intent that counts. It is the result.

THE PURPOSE OF ART

Now, a problem: Serving someone else is the answer—but not always. How about a visual artist? Whom is she serving? Let's say this artist never exhibits her work, thus never enriches the society or community with new aspects of artistic expression that others will study.

What about performing artists? Whom are they serving? If they decline to "commercialize"—i.e., focus on what the audience wants to see or hear— then they serve their art, their own inner light, which is the most demanding master there is. They lose themselves when they work. They lose all sense of time and space.

What about non-commercial fine artists? Let's say they refuse to consciously cater to the prevalent tastes of the audience; on the contrary, they expect the audience to adapt to their art. Are *they* self-serving to the point of being a cancer?

Not at all. I once read a play by Tagore, the Indian poet. In it, the king challenges an artist, asking: "Who needs you?" The artist responds: "Imagine the world without us. Then you will know our value."

If you lose a cancer, you do not miss it, do you? But if you lose art, you *will* miss it. That is the difference.

Fine artists serve society by just being what they are—by being agents of change, even without intending to be.

It is not the intent that counts. It is the result of your life's work.

As long as you add value, whether it is by serving others or by serving the needs of society at large by just being present, you are effective, whether you intend to be or not. This is about the impact you have. It is what remains after you are gone, since others were affected by what you did. That is called being effective, and when you live an effective life, you do not die. Your deeds remain to remind us of your presence.

THE BENEFITS OF
SLOWING DOWN[1]

W E live in a hectic world that is becoming more and more hectic all the time.

We have more and more problems and opportunities that demand our attention. Our minds are more and more at work. The result is that from the moment we wake up until we go to sleep, our minds are fully engaged and our eyes are focused on what is going on inside. We wake up and the next thing we know we are having supper and are ready to sleep.

Where did the day go? It went between our ears: As our brains became and remained fully engaged—analyzing the past, understanding why we have problems, and building scenarios for how to solve problems or exploit opportunities in the future—we were so busy inside our heads that we did not notice the smile of the baby, the blooming of the roses, or how the wind was caressing our faces.

In the future, we will have no memory of our children crawling, our loved ones crying, or our garden blooming. We saw these things, but we did not register them, because our eyes were focused inward, watching ourselves deal with the past or future—and missing the present.

Because of medical advances, we live longer chronologically, but experience life as being very short. I, for one, feel that Christmas is arriving sooner every year. When the piped Christmas music starts playing, I always wonder how the year passed by so fast.

Why? Where did life go? Between our ears, with our eyes turned inward.

We were solving problems, rushing from one agenda item to the next without a break in-between.

Eventually, all our days start looking the same: We get up, we run, run,

---

[1] Adizes Insights, December 11, 2009.

run, we go home, we go to sleep (assuming that we succeed in falling asleep). Eventually we won't know what day of the week—or even which year—it is.

The day may come that we will graduate from school, go to work—and the next thing we will be aware of is that we are gasping for air, because we are dying.

SMELL THE ROSES—NO, REALLY!

Many well-meaning people tell us to stop rushing through life, to take time to smell the flowers. It is a great recommendation, but *how?*

Is it as simple as canceling a meeting and going for a walk in the garden? No! We can cancel many meetings, walk in many gardens, and even smell the flowers ... and still have no memory of it—unless....

My insight is that in order to *smell* the flowers, we need to *see* them first. We need to become aware of their existence and beauty, and for that we need to turn our eyes outward. And that will only happen when we stop our brains from totally monopolizing our awareness.

We need to slow our minds. We need to control our minds, rather than be controlled by them.

We need to move from the brain to the heart.

What do I mean by that?

LET YOUR HEART SPEAK

The brain has left and right sides to it. The right side is very liberal, creative, and risk-taking. The left side is detail-oriented, risk-averse, and conservative. The two halves of your brain can spend days, even years, arguing with each other about what to do—and leaving you totally bewildered. You will make decisions and act, because you have to—but you will be full of doubts, burdened by anxiety and worry.

When you listen to your heart, it is like being in love. When you make a decision "with all your heart," there is no doubt, no anxiety, no worry. You feel at peace with your decision. You don't continually have to ask yourself, "Why?"

Granted, with any problem, you should *start* thinking with your brain; do your due diligence on the issue. But end your internal debates with your heart. When it is time to make a final decision, let your heart speak.

Your heart will have a chance to be heard only when you tell your brain that enough is enough and it is time to shut up.

To be freed from the "brain master" that enslaves you, you need to be above it, to have it under control. You should not let it overcome you and thus drive you. The same is true with emotions: Of course it is OK to have them, but they must be kept under control. And the same applies to your body and its urges.

Who is the boss? You. And who are "you"? "You" are neither your mind, nor your body, nor your emotions, nor your spirit. You are above them all. Your spirit dwells in your heart, while your mind is in your brain and your emotions in your liver.

> You are neither your mind, nor your body, nor your emotions, nor your spirit.

When we finalize decisions based on what our hearts tell us, we feel complete. And when that happens, our lives will be filled with love instead of being filled with doubts. Life will be less stressful and more enjoyable. We will feel as though we live longer, with more memories and fewer disappointments.

How can we slow our minds down and get all of these benefits?

Ask me and I will tell you.

With all my heart.

THE BENEFITS OF
DOING NOTHING[1]

EVERY day in the modern world, the number of problems and opportunities in our lives increases. There are so many oppor-threats, both existing and new, that we simply don't have time to address them all. We are all busy, and if we stop for even a second, we feel guilty, because we know that there is so much to do.

But you might find that there are benefits to stopping for an interval of time and just doing nothing.

First, doing nothing gives you time to review what you are engaged in and analyze whether or not you should continue doing it. Are you accomplishing your original goal?

Doing nothing is like pulling yourself out of a picture so that you can see the picture from a different perspective. We all know how difficult it is to see the picture when you are in it. Stepping outside of it makes it possible to see the value, or the futility, of what you are doing.

We also know that filling our time with activity is a perfect escape from ourselves, while doing nothing forces us, sometimes painfully, to face ourselves and our concerns.

When you do nothing, you have an opportunity to reminisce and to ask yourself, "Is it time to change?"

ZERO AND INFINITY ARE RELATED

I have noticed an interesting phenomenon among people who have asked for a divorce: I ask them when the idea of divorce began to germinate, and when did they make the final decision to make a change? Often, it happened when they were on vacation, or sick in bed with nothing to do. With nothing

---

[1] Adizes Insights, April 2009.

to do, they had the time to evaluate the past and make plans for the future.

In the Hindu tradition, zero and infinity are related. Everything is nothing. Nothing is everything. Dedicating an interval of time to doing nothing provides space for creating something new. When your brain is otherwise engaged, it is not available to be creative.

I have found an interesting common denominator among my entrepreneurial clients: When they were young, they often found themselves alone with nothing to do, either because they were ill or for some other reason.

> *Doing nothing is a science and an art.*

Having nothing to do, they had to create something by themselves. They did lots of daydreaming, and over time they developed their dream and made it a reality.

TO CHANGE TRACKS, IT IS NECESSARY TO SLOW DOWN

What I have been saying so far boils down to this: Having nothing to do is a prerequisite for making a change. Have you ever suddenly found the resolve to make a strategic change when you were stressed trying to catch a plane? I don't think so.

Look at a train. To change the rails it is riding on, it needs to slow down or even stop altogether. Full speed ahead and changing direction are not compatible activities. (P) and (E) are incompatible roles. You need (I) in the middle to enable change.[2]

Having nothing to do can create the opportunity to make a strategic change in your life. What may seem to be a problem could be a blessing in disguise.

Many entrepreneurs, for example, started their companies after being fired from their previous jobs and having nothing to do for a while. Before that, being employed, and struggling to remain employed, used all the limited energy they had; they simply didn't have energy to think about starting a business. Getting fired was the best thing that could have happened to them. It gave them the time and energy to analyze what they really wanted to do with their lives and what strategic changes they wanted to make.

Recession might also be a blessing in disguise. Falling sales, falling

---

[2] For further details about the (PAEI) code, see my book *The Ideal Executive: Why You Cannot Be One and What to Do About It* (Santa Barbara, CA: Adizes Institute Publications, 2004).

production, and less pressure to fulfill orders all provide a window of opportunity for decision-makers to re-evaluate the past and implement strategic changes for the future.

BUT WHAT COUNTS AS DOING NOTHING?

Now a word of warning: Watching TV or reading a book in the shade of your sun umbrella, or swimming, or surfing, or biking … none of these count as doing nothing. They could be classified as "vacation," but not as "doing nothing."

"Nothing" means *nothing*. "Nothing" means having no agenda, no goal to achieve, nothing that engages your mind in any way. "Nothing" means that your mind is allowed to be free to wander.

In yoga, lying relaxed on the floor (the "dead man pose") is considered a pose in itself—and a very important one. Knowing how to do nothing is a science and an art.

How, then, should you go about doing nothing?

Here is what I believe: You will never *find* the time to do nothing; you have to consciously and intentionally *take* the time to do nothing.

The easiest way to implement this philosophy of life is to meditate. I meditate twice a day for an hour.

If you do not want to meditate, make a commitment to sit and do nothing every day for an hour without feeling guilty about it. Have a pad and pen available; you may be surprised by what you think up.

Doing nothing is doing something very important. It enables you to change, and in the hectic world in which we live, change is a prerequisite for success.

INSIGHTS FROM REIKI[1]

S OME time ago I took a course in Reiki, which is a method of moving
energy in the body for the purpose of healing.

I wanted to see if I could learn from this method: Was it possible to move
the energy of companies and, by doing so, heal them?

I did get some insights. Here they are:

DESTINY

Reiki says that all human beings have a destiny. How do we discover
what our destiny is? By listening to the "call," and by not turning away from
that "call."

How do you know what the "call" is?

Here is the insight: When you respond to the call, you *get* energy. When
you do something else, you *lose* energy.

When you respond to the call, you accept your destiny, your purpose in
life. You are inspired. You are integrated with something larger than yourself,
that absolute consciousness that people call God.

When I was studying for my Ph.D., I had to choose which field I would
specialize in. At that time, operations research was in vogue. Management as
a field of study was in decline, I was warned—there was not enough rigorous
mathematical modeling. It was too soft. Everyone recommended that I keep
away from it. "There are no jobs teaching management," I was told.

But in my heart, I knew that was what I loved. Thinking about why
and how things happen in organizations is what keeps me awake at night
and gives me pleasure. I followed my "call" and did what my heart—not my
head—told me to do.

And I did the right thing. I have never "worked"; I am always in wonder
that people are willing to pay me for having the pleasure of helping them solve

[1] Adizes Insights, April 2006.

their problems. When I lecture or write or consult, I have more energy at the end of the day than when I started. It is as if God rewards me for serving a purpose I was born to serve.

Think of a machine, designed for a specific purpose and used for that purpose. When you are not following your destiny, it is as if you are misusing the machine. You are using a vacuum cleaner to clean your pool instead of your carpets.

I lose energy if I have to do accounting or deal with my staff's problems. I like to observe, study, write, and lecture about management; but do not ask me to actually manage. I am like an art critic; must I be a good artist, too?

THE FIVE RULES OF REIKI

Just for today, do not worry.
Just for today, do not be angry.
Honor your parents and teachers and elders.
Do your job with integrity.
Have gratitude.[2]

DO NOT WORRY

Worry is future-oriented. It is what you *want* to happen, without knowing whether it *will* happen. That is why you are worried. But the future has not happened yet, and your worries might not be realized.

Worry is also past-oriented: "I should have done something, but I didn't." "I should not have smoked, but I did."

You cannot undo the past. So what need is there to worry about it? Learn from the past, and apply what you have learned to the future.

Do not ask yourself *why* something happened. Ask yourself *for what* did it happen. This question will prompt you to learn, because "for what?" prompts you to ask if there is a purpose to your experience; what were you supposed to learn from it?

Worry takes energy away. It is "internal marketing." Not worrying means to have faith that: a) I can learn from my past; and b) I can handle the future when it arrives.

---

[2] Mikao Usui, *The Original Reiki Handbook* (Twin Lakes, WI: Lotus Press, 1999).

It is interesting to note that truly religious people, of any religion, tend to be more peaceful. They believe that "God will provide" and "God will forgive."

Those who are not religious carry the terrible burden of having to forgive themselves and having to handle alone all the problems that come their way. Omnipotence is a good feeling, but also a great burden.

Now note that Reiki does not say: Don't worry. It says: "Just for *today*, do not worry." Hmmm ... If every day you say, "Just for today, I am not going to worry," then you will *never* worry, because there is nothing more permanent than continuous temporary. Just take one day at a time and have the discipline to repeat your commitment. You are not *committing* for a lifetime, but you are *acting* for a lifetime. One day at a time. How should you eat a salami? One slice at a time. And how do you eat an elephant? Also one bite at a time.

DO NOT BE ANGRY

Anger is caused by fear.

Think about it.

Each time you are angry, ask yourself what it is that you fear. If you remove the fear, you will remove the anger.

Some time ago I was walking with my dog on the beach, where there were many other dogs. I had him on a leash. My friend told me to let him off the leash. "But he will attack the other dogs," I said.

"Just the opposite," he said. "When a dog is on a leash, it feels weak and scared; and when another dog approaches, it will attack first out of fear of getting hurt."

Hmmm... I thought to myself. That must be why the prophet Daniel walked into a lion's cage and nothing happened to him. He had no fear. He had faith in God.

> Just for today, do not worry.
> Just for today, do not be angry.
> Honor your parents and teachers and elders.
> Do your job with integrity.
> Have gratitude.

When we fear, we attack proactively to defend ourselves. That attack is called "anger."

So rules 1 and 2 mean to have faith and to have no fear—just for today. And if you do it every day, guess what? You will never be angry or fearful.

Honor Your Parents and Teachers

This is also one of the Ten Commandments.

The Hebrew language has two different words denoting respect: one means, literally, "honor," and the other means "value."

Honor is how you behave—not what you think. Value is what you think.

In Hebrew, the word *kavod* for "honor" comes from the word *kaved* for "heavy." To honor means to recognize someone's "weight," or substance. For example, when a woman loses her honor, it is as if she's lost weight, but not physically; it is more like losing her good will. A dishonorable man is one who does not keep his word. It is as if he has no anchor to hold his ship in place, nothing to hold onto. He is too light. You cannot rely on such a person. When a family defends its honor, it is defending its brand name, its good will, its assets in the marketplace.

So what does it mean to "honor your parents"? It means to recognize the assets they are giving you. You did not start from zero. You belong to some brand. They gave you something. You are the continuation of that something. You are starting where they are ending. So can you recognize that and be thankful? That is why you bow and hold your palms together when you honor: You are acknowledging and thanking them for what you've received. The same applies to teachers.

Teachers and parents "teach" you, which means they try to "change" you; and that is painful. It is tough to accept pain and still value it.

Thus, neither Reiki nor the Bible asks us to decide whether or not we value our parents. It commands us to behave in a certain way: to honor our parents and teachers regardless of what we think. Whether we value them or not, we should behave *as if* we do.

In the (PAEI) code, this would be (A) behavior that is being prescribed here, not (E) or (I).[3] And it fits with my experience. In the Adizes methodology, we insist that people behave as if they respect each other even if in fact they do *not* value each other's contributions. You do not know what value people give you until the discussion is over, and even then it is not clear who is right. Therefore, it does not make sense to discount the value people give you *a priori*.

---

[3] For more details about the (PAEI) code, see my book *The Ideal Executive: Why You Cannot Be One and What to Do About It* (Santa Barbara, CA: Adizes Institute Publications, 2004).

Why don't Reiki and the Bible say: "Love your parents"?

Because love is an (I) phenomenon: No one—not even God—can make you love anyone. But you *can* honor. You can *behave* respectfully. It is form that creates the function, rather than relying on the function to create the form.

Behave honorably—at all times and in all cases. Do not prejudge whether others deserve it or not.

DO YOUR JOB WITH INTEGRITY

Again, this principle has to do with internal marketing. When a person has integrity, there is no difference between what he does and what he believes he should do. When you have integrity, you are integrated, you are one: What you *want*, what you *should* do, and what you *do* are one and the same. No doubts. No frustration. No sleepless nights. You are at peace with yourself.

HAVE GRATITUDE

In Adizes language, this is called Reinforcement. It also is the final integration. You are thankful for whatever happens to you. You do not worry about rejection. You do not suffer from denial, anger, or worry.

These five rules together serve to eliminate internal conflicts in a person. Such a person will suffer no internal disintegration, and therefore can be an effective healer—of a person or an organization.

Why?

Because disease is caused by disintegration. "To heal" means to make whole. Disease uses energy; a sick system loses

> When you respond to the "call," you accept your destiny, your purpose in life. You are inspired.

energy. Healing requires bringing energy from the outside or releasing it from wherever it got stuck. So a healer gives energy to the sick person. The more energy the healer can give, the better he is as a healer.

If people are internally disintegrated, most of their energy goes to treating themselves, and very little is left to heal others. In the worst-case scenario, a so-called "healer" uses the energy of his patient to help himself. That is called abuse.

But when you have no internal conflicts sapping your energy, you can give love—and love heals.

Jesus was a great healer, apparently because he had no internal conflicts whatsoever. The same was true of Buddha.

IMPLICATIONS FOR BEING A BETTER ADIZES CERTIFIED ASSOCIATE

Before you go to work with a client, meditate for twenty minutes. Get yourself together.

Next, remove all worries and fears.

Doing your job with integrity means that if you do what you *should* do and *want* to do, then what you *are* doing will not create conflicts and disintegration between your mind and your emotions.

Honoring your teachers means giving credit to those whose work you are using. Do not usurp brand or intellectual property.

And last, show gratitude to your profession, no matter what happens. Being an Adizes Associate should be a calling, not a job. Have gratitude that you are doing that which not only heals your clients but also gives you energy.

Be one who helps others become one.

ON MEDITATION[1]

I N the spring of 2008, I spent two weeks in India, following a meditation guru from town to town, two days per location.

This was my fourth visit to India, but I consider it the first real one. The other three were too touristy. Two were lecture tours: I stayed in the best hotels, with hot water and all the excellent services money can buy. The third was for a *Maha Kumbh Mela*, which is a gathering of Hindus on the Ganges River every 144 years. Sadhus (mystics or ascetics) descend from their caves in the Himalayas, and it is "a freak show," as Sunil, one of my Indian associates, described it. Granted, it was interesting to see the fakirs, but it was not every-day India.

This time, it *was* the real India. I slept in an ashram, was driven from town to town in terrible traffic, ate with Indians on the floor and meditated with them. At my age (71), it was not an easy experience, but the guru was even older (80-something) and *he* held on well, so who was I to complain?

What did I learn?

The meditation opened my eyes to understanding mysteries I have struggled for years to understand.

The meditation I was practicing is called *Sahaj Marg*, which means "the natural way." The practice is to focus on and listen to the heart, by slowing down the mind. No mantra; no focusing on the breath or on a candle or whatever. Just the heart.

I joined this type of practice because I believed I needed it the most. First, being Jewish, I spend most of my time in my head, and it needed a rest; second, because I saw my dearest relatives and friends sent to their deaths during World War II, which closed my heart for all these years. It needed re-opening.

---

[1] Adizes Insights, June 2008.

LISTEN TO YOUR HEART

Now, here is one of the many valuable insights I got from meditation:

How do you know, when you meditate, which thoughts are of the mind and which are of the heart? Thoughts are thoughts, no?

No. There is a difference. Thoughts of the mind you can argue with, and you do: You toss and turn and debate with yourself over them. But when your heart "speaks," there is no argument. There is no discussion. There is no "Why?" or "Why not?" You are complete; you are at peace with yourself. To the question "Why?" the answer is "Because," and that's it. Think of how you feel when you are in love with all your heart. There are no doubts, right? You are completely "sold"!

That brought me to the next insight: *If you really listen to your heart when you need to make a decision, but your heart is silent, it means you are not ready to finalize your decision.* The fruit is not ripe yet; leave it on the branch to ripen. This is a case when it is better *not* to decide than to decide too quickly.

Next interesting insight from meditating: *When you decide with your heart, you cannot make a mistake.*

Why not?

Well, what *is* a mistake? It is always a conclusion you come to after the fact. Right? It is a feeling of remorse and a judgment that you should have decided differently. It is something you figure out only after the fact, and it leads to self-accusations that perhaps you did not deliberate enough, that you did not listen to advice, that you ignored facts, etc.

But when you make a decision with your heart, you are at peace with yourself. Even if you discover, after the fact, that your decision did not work out as you expected, you do not feel remorse, because at the time you made that decision you had no doubts about it; therefore you could not have done any better. The mistake is of academic interest: What can be learned from what happened? But there is no place for remorse. You were at peace when you decided, and it is what it is.

THE BENEFITS OF MEDITATING

How do you come to such peace of mind, especially if there is a difficult decision to be made? You can only do it by meditating. And that is where the most important insight is: *When you meditate, do not get attached to thoughts.*

That way, you will not get into endless arguments with yourself. And as you let your thoughts pass through you, like clouds in the sky, your heart will speak.

The heart speaks only when there is silence. That is why we seem to fall in love more often in times of peace and quiet. I have never met a person who fell in love when he was stressed. You need to quiet your mind, to give time and space for the heart to speak.

THE MANY VOICES

Let me share with you a story, told to me by my associate Prof. Will McWhinney, that I hope will demonstrate this point.

When McWhinney was a student at Yale, the fraternities held a contest for best choir. McWhinney's fraternity had the worst voices at the university—except for one person, whose voice was a pure, evangelical tenor.

So they devised the following performance: The whole choir got on stage and began to sing, but each person sang a different melody, which produced total cacophony. Then, slowly, one by one, they stopped singing. Meanwhile, the beautiful voice of the tenor became stronger and stronger, until it was alone, pure and crystal clear and totally enchanting.

They won first prize.

The same thing happens in meditation. You have many voices in your head, all competing with each other. The more difficult the decision is, the more voices you will hear and the more stress you will experience because of all that noise.

When you meditate, you shut the voices down, one by one, while your heart's "voice" grows stronger and stronger, until you simply "hear" the answer to your question and feel at peace with your decision.

Yoga teachers say the mind is a terrorist. It terrorizes us. I once saw a bumper sticker that said, "Do not always believe what you think."

Now think about *that*.

The Destructive
Nature of (E)-Types[1]

I AM in Israel. I can't get over how much this country has advanced. I often tell people, "America is *here*"—"America" meaning "bounty," "good quality of life," etc.

Still, everyone here complains endlessly. It's as if they are all looking for something to complain about.

Which reminds me of a joke:

"What does a waiter say to a table full of old Jewish ladies?

"Is *anything* OK?"

Come to think of it, I have never, ever been to Israel—and I have been coming here at least once a year for the last forty-seven years—when people were not complaining about how terrible Israel is in some way or other.

Then it occurred to me that it is not just Israelis who complain. It is Jews. They are never happy. My Jewish clients, no matter how successful they are, bitch and moan and endlessly complain.

But when I thought about it some more, I realized that this phenomenon of not being happy is not only a Jewish characteristic. It is also true of all the (E)-types I know. It just happens that Jewish people are more (E)-oriented than others.

Aha! It seems that what drives (E)s to cause change—and often it's change for the sake of change—is a deep dissatisfaction, a sense of being "incomplete," or not content with themselves.

When an (E) feels unhappy with himself, he tries to fill that emptiness by making changes "out there"—building business empires, starting a political revolution, or being the best research scientist alive.

That is how (E)s end up leading change.

---

[1] Adizes Insights, December 2010.

We (E)s are unhappy people who try to find peace and happiness outside ourselves, when the truth is that we can only find peace and happiness within us.

So what does this mean?

My first conclusion, as an organizational therapist, is that from now on I should take the (E)s' perpetual complaints with a grain of salt. I will take them less seriously and also make sure I don't get so depressed about it that I become an ineffective consultant who never succeeds in bringing my client to self-fulfillment and satisfaction.

> We (E)s are unhappy people who try to find peace and happiness outside ourselves.

Instead, I need to take their accusations about my inadequacies as a manifestation of their inner struggles with themselves. And I must learn to differentiate between real problems and my clients' *need* to have a problem.

Finally, I must remember to let my (E) clients hold onto at least one of their problems—otherwise they will feel less alive.

And come to think of it, this conclusion applies to me, too!

ON BEING JEWISH[1]

I JUST finished a book I could not put down until the last page: *Treblinka*, by Jean-Francois Steiner. Originally published in French in 1966, it has been translated into sixteen languages. Simon & Schuster first published the English translation in 1967.

The book is a kind of diary of what happened in Treblinka, the extermination camp where nearly one million Jews were gassed and their bodies burned to ashes to erase all traces of the atrocities. Among the victims were my grandmother, grandfather, three uncles, three aunts, and six cousins.

What I found extraordinary were the author's insights about the essence of the Jewish psyche—of being Jewish.

Often, in reading a book, you find that one valuable sentence justifies having read the other hundreds of pages. This book offers a lot more than one sentence.

Take the following, from a passage in which the author explains why most Jews—millions of them—went to their deaths without a fight.

Here is his explanation: "It is not truth that mattered the most, but hope."

This sentence explained many of the mysteries I have encountered in trying to understand Jewish behavior in general.

On one hand, we Jews debate any item with passion, turning the subject over and over, attacking it from every angle as if committed to finding the absolute, undeniable truth. (Which, by the way, we never do find, even though we've been arguing for thousands of years.)

But this behavior pertains to the intellectual realm. When the subject is of personal or emotional significance, we do the opposite: We bury our heads in the sand, refusing to recognize reality (truth), and clinging to hope beyond rationality.

---

[1] Adizes Insights, September 2010.

'EVERYTHING WILL BE ALL RIGHT'

When I ask Israelis what their plan is for dealing with a complicated problem, often the typical answer is: "*Yihye beseder*"—"Everything will be all right." Period. "Just relax; it will be fine!"

In a CBS-TV interview in October 1956, Ben Gurion, the first Prime Minister of Israel, was asked if he hoped for miracles to keep Israel alive. He replied: "In Israel, in order to be a realist you must believe in miracles."

On Passover night for thousands of years, every Jew recites, "Next year in Jerusalem." Even if he is in a dungeon, sentenced to die the next morning: "Next year in Jerusalem."

And what is the song sung in synagogues worldwide, that Israel adopted as its national anthem? "*Hatikvah*"!—"The Hope." Here is the refrain (English translation):

> *Jews have the hardest time making decisions because they always see more facets to a problem than are necessary to solve it.*

"Our hope is not yet lost,
The hope of two thousand years,
To be a free people in our land,
The land of Zion and Jerusalem."

Israel has been free for more than sixty years, and yet we are still singing that refrain. What do we hope for now?

Hope is related to faith—faith that no matter what, we will survive.

Here is the most famous passage of the Old Testament's 23rd Psalm: "Though I walk through the valley of the shadow of death, I have no fear, because God is with me."

We are the chosen people. We will survive. Hope, always hope, and faith will dominate our behavior—not the reality of how desperate the situation might be.

On one hand, hope has beneficial value, because we never yield; we never surrender to despair. But on the other hand, an unrealistic hope lulls many of us into a false state of security. As a result, we do not react in a timely fashion to the dangers facing us. As an example, most Jews did not fight back when they were forced into the gas chambers. They did not escape in time. We clung to any sign of hope, no matter how improbable.

Are we better now, more realistic in our behavior?

NEVER SATISFIED WITH THE POSSIBLE

Another sentence in *Treblinka* reinforced my experiences working as a consultant for Israeli and many other Jewish companies. Steiner referred to "the typical Jewish quality of always looking for the hardest way, always wanting to do better, never being satisfied with the possible, and undertaking against all odds what is logically impossible."

This might explain why our ratio of Nobel Prize-winners per capita is the highest in the world. But it has its emotional liabilities.

It is not easy consulting to Jewish companies. They always claim to know better, are never satisfied with what I or they or we or anyone else did. There is always someone who says, "Yes, but you could also have…."

Jews have the hardest time making decisions because they always see more facets to a problem than are necessary to solve it. They enjoy the type of debate called *pilpul* (derived from the word *pilpel*—or pepper, for the sharp intellectual battle you wage to prove your point), which they engage in for its own sake, the sake of sharpening their argumentative capabilities, not necessarily for solving the problem.

In the United States, I find that my non-Jewish clients take a complicated problem and work on simplifying it in order to solve it.

My Jewish clients—anywhere in the world—do the opposite. They take a simple problem and through endless debate make it so unnecessarily complicated that often it starts to look too complicated to solve.

Results are not what excite them. On the contrary, it is the *pilpul*, the debate, and the process of seeing all angles plus one of any issue that they enjoy.

The result of it all is that we are never satisfied, never content for too long. To be satisfied, apparently, is anathema to being Jewish.

I strongly recommend this book. Read it and form your own judgment. I hope to hear your reactions.

WISHES FOR THE NEW YEAR[1]

H ERE we are, facing another New Year, another opportunity for wishful thinking ... *unless* this year, perhaps, we can change the old pattern and really commit ourselves to action. Because without positive action, whatever we have today will be worse tomorrow by default.

What are you committed to changing in the coming year? And how will you make sure that this time it isn't just wishful thinking?

Change necessarily means moving from one condition to another, and abandoning the old condition means sacrificing something. Whether we are aware of it or not, the old condition must have had certain rewards; otherwise we would not have embraced it for so long. We can measure the degree of our commitment by the degree of sacrifice we are willing to make.

What are "New Year's resolutions"? They are the hopes and wishes we make for ourselves. But sadly, they are wishes we rarely act on, because although we want something new, we never really commit to giving up the benefits of the old.

Take me, for example. In the coming new year, I am committed to losing twenty more pounds; to stop working on Saturdays; and to spend no more than ten days a month consulting, so that I have more time to write books. And here is what I am willing to sacrifice: the pleasure of food, and a significant portion of my personal income.

Why am I writing about my own New Year's wishes, instead of wishing you a productive and profitable year? Because I find that the most difficult commitments to fulfill are the ones we make to ourselves. It is so much easier to break the promises I made to myself than the ones I pledged to others.

So: In the coming year, may you fulfill the promises you made to yourself, and find the strength to make the sacrifices needed to make your commitment real. Amen.

---

[1] Adizes Insights, January 2010.

PART 2

HEALTHY LIVING
AND
UNHEALTHY LIVING

The New Jungle (Part 1)[1]

I N the Stone Age, the fittest survived. But what exactly does "the fittest" mean? It was an era of scarcity, so whoever was the strongest, or could hunt better, or run faster, survived—and if he could reproduce, his genes survived. The common denominator was physical ability. In that era, it was easy to identify the enemy, whether it was a wolf, a lion, or a competing tribe.

But now I think we live in an era of a new kind of "jungle," a jungle of our own making, which requires completely different skills for survival. In the modern era, it has become very difficult to identify the enemy, and the strongest is no longer necessarily the fittest.

We, in the developed parts of the world, live not in an era of scarcity but of abundance. Just look at any supermarket in the developed world. There are so many foods to choose from. But is any of it good for us? Is it healthy? Research done by a supermarket chain found that if you eliminate the produce department—which is what nature provides and which is by definition healthy—76 percent of the 24,000 items the supermarket sells have no nutritional value.[2]

Enemies in Friendly Packages

In the Stone Age, a snake was a snake and a lion was a lion. There was no mistaking where the threat was coming from. Today, fast food, sugary drinks, and animal products (dairy and meat) loaded with fat and antibiotics are packaged and promoted as if they were the best things for us to eat. And slowly, they are killing us.

This life-threatening lifestyle is promoted by corporate advertisements that use the most sophisticated, well-researched psychological methods to convince us to consume foods that are bad for us.

---

[1] Adizes Insights, July 2009.

[2] Data provided by Dr. Jeff Novack of the Pritikin Center.

A shocking number of people in developed countries die prematurely from heart attacks, strokes, cancer, and diabetes: diseases associated with a lifestyle that includes very little exercise, working in a stressful environment, and consuming food that clogs arteries and causes inflammation—in other words, most commercial, packaged food products.

In the new jungle, the enemy is parading as a friend. In the new jungle, people may consume toxic food and not even know it is harmful. We are falling apart and don't even realize it.

WHO ARE THE FITTEST NOW?

So who will survive in this new jungle? Not the strongest physically. Nor the most intelligent. I suggest to you that it will be those with the self-discipline to say "No!" to temptations; those who have the willpower and discipline to select very carefully what they eat; those who take the time to exercise and rest sufficiently.

People who believe that bigger muscles and lots of exercise will prolong their lives, but who, at the same time, eat junk food, are not doing themselves much good.

We all know it is not easy to say no. The temptations are enormous. Fast-food outlets are everywhere; opportunities to work more and rest less are infinite. And as this way of living continues to make us sick, drug companies continue to develop drugs to overcome the diseases created by our lifestyle—only to create new health problems from those drugs' side effects.

Who will survive? Those who are conscious and have self-discipline and willpower. We're not in the Stone Age anymore. What counts is *not* how fast you run, but how tightly you close your mouth.

THE NEW JUNGLE (PART 2)[1]

I AM concerned by the ways in which modern life disempowers us through addictions: to unhealthy food, technology, drugs, dangerous pleasures—and who knows what will be next?

The conclusion I have arrived at is that the people who will survive are no longer going to be those who can adapt. Darwin's theory of adaptation might even be dangerous now; it implies that we *should* adapt to new technologies, drugs, and foods. But I believe this is the wrong adaptation, which could eventually reduce our long-term happiness and shorten our lives.

Those who survive will be the ones who swim against the current—those who have the power and the self-discipline to say "No!" to the toxic foods, drugs, and technologies that are continually being offered—"No!" to the endless temptations and pleasures that, in the long run, will end in misery.

In short, those who survive will be the ones who do *not* adapt.

SAYING 'YES!' DOESN'T WORK

But how do we develop this self-discipline, this power to say "No"? Is it not better instead to say "Yes!"—"Yes!" to exercise, instead of "No!" to sitting in front of the TV all day; "Yes!" to a nutritious diet, instead of "No!" to oily fast food; "Yes!" to a healthy lifestyle in general?

No.

I have found from experience that "Yes!" does not work very well, because the temptations, the addictions, are strong. Imagine a drug addict being offered his drug of choice and yet choosing to say "Yes!" to good health instead. It won't work. He needs to have the willpower to say "No!" to the drugs. We all need to be able to say "No!" and actually walk our talk.

I am training myself to say "No!" First, I started counting how many times a day I said "No!" to unhealthy temptations, and how many times

[1] Adizes Insights, July 2009.

I failed to say "No!," and I am trying to improve that ratio. I am trying to figure out an appropriate reward for myself at the end of the week for being self-disciplined.

THE ADVANTAGE OF RELIGION

I am truly envious of religious Jews who honor the Sabbath: no work, no phones, no BlackBerrys, no driving, no television or radio. Pure peace. They have time to reconnect with their families and themselves, to reconnect with their spiritual convictions.

Think of it: What is the difference between humans and animals? Animals do not discriminate between *kodesh ve hol*—between the sacred and the non-sacred. Every day is the same for them. They recognize seasons, but only because nature forces them to, not because of a choice they make.

But humans have a Sabbath, or Christmas, or Yom Kippur, or Ramadan. They choose to behave differently at certain times.

The modern world, with all its temptations, is increasingly making us animalistic: Driven by our addictions and external forces, we are losing our willpower to self-direct. Because we increasingly choose to work on sacred days, we make all days the same. The result is that time flies: the years feel shorter, and consequently life also feels shorter, even though our life span is actually longer than our ancestors'.

Every year, Rosh Hashanah and Yom Kipper, Judaism's holiest days, seem to arrive faster and faster. New Year's Eve was not last year, I think to myself, but last week. How did a whole year pass by? Where did the time go?

The more we say "Yes!," the faster the wheel of life spins and the shorter is the span of life we enjoy.

We must stop. Take a break. Say "No!" to phones, Twitter, blogs, BlackBerrys, TV, driving, shopping, to whatever else we do six days a week. One day of every week should be a "No!" day.

For myself, I am committed to making Saturdays a day of rest. No phones. No TV. No driving.

Unfortunately, I don't find going to the synagogue fulfilling; neither the rituals nor the prayers speak to me. So what to do instead? I tried reading the weekend newspapers, but the newspapers kept repeating themselves and, worse, they depressed me. Exercise? That's good, but that should be done every day.

Then I found the answer: When I read books that make me wiser, I feel rejuvenated at the end of the day. So I have been reading Osho, the famous Indian spiritual teacher. And when I get tired of him, I read *Pirkey Avot*, the Jewish book of wisdom. I am going to read books of wisdom from all religions.

I also read books of jokes; there is a lot of wisdom in some of them.

The Sabbath day, the "No!" day (and it does not have to be Saturday, it can be any day you choose), is your day to take it absolutely slow and easy: long, long meals; talk to your spouse without allowing interruptions or phone calls or appointments; and no driving anyone anywhere.

I wish there could be a new religion, the religion of "No!" We could wear a pin that says "No!" on our lapels so we could recognize and support each other in standing up to modern addictions.

ENFORCE THAT 'NO!'

I hope we can teach our children how to say "No!," not only to drugs, but also to violent computer games, obesity-causing fast-food outlets, and obsessive TV watching. That is the kind of character-building that future generations need, if we are going to survive as a civilization.

I believe our ancestors knew how to say "No!" better than we do today, and were better able to tell their children "No!" than we are today.

Today, in two-career families, no one has the energy to say and enforce a "No!" to the temptations our children are increasingly exposed to. In fact, there is more "No!" that needs to be said, but less time and willpower to enforce it—particularly when we are constantly being bombarded by permissive theories of "self-actualization" and "freedom of choice"—jargon that is often used as an excuse to avoid setting and enforcing boundaries. Consequently, our children are lost in a jungle of pleasure traps, with dangerous long-term consequences.

> We are training the whole world to feel guilty, as we do, if we stop to smell the flowers.

And I do not foresee a better future. As I travel around the world and observe how developing countries are trying to emulate the West, I feel sorry for the lifestyle they are losing. We try to convince the Chinese to save less and spend more, to increase consumer debt. We spread our fast food and sugary drinks everywhere. We promote our Protestant work ethic, which puts work ahead of all other values. We are training the whole world to feel guilty, as we do, if we stop to smell the flowers.

Let us practice saying "No!"

"No!" "No!" "No!"

And again: "No!"

Why I am 'Pro-Life'

THE modern phenomenon of sexual freedom has meant that pregnancies among unmarried women have increased dramatically. Given that such pregnancies are often unplanned and unwelcome, how should our society regard this problem?

At first blush, legalizing abortions seems to be the only viable option. Those who support free choice point out that even if abortions became illegal, that would not stop abortions. Abortions would continue to be performed, but by non-professionals and criminals, potentially with coat hangers, endangering women's lives.

This brings us to the second argument for legalizing abortion: that a woman should have the right to choose what happens to her body.

A third argument is that, in any case, a fetus in the womb is not really "alive," not yet a human being—that it does not feel pain or have a spirit or consciousness. (According to this argument, a fetus is a lot like a vegetable.)

DEFINING THE PROBLEM

But does legalizing abortion address the problem, or does it merely address a manifestation of the problem?

And is the easy solution necessarily the *right* solution?

The "dark-alley," "coat-hanger" argument does not convince me. Dark alleys and coat hangers are also manifestations of the problem.

Here is the problem: Our promiscuous culture, supported and promoted by the media, creates an environment that promotes promiscuous sex, which causes unwanted pregnancies. Sex sells, and the people who promote sex make billions, while some of those infatuated with it end up in dark alleys.

Let us attack the roots of the problem—the commercialization of sex—instead of just the "leaves"—the unwanted pregnancies.

I am equally unconvinced by the second argument, that women should have control over their bodies. If women should have control over their bodies, shouldn't they also control their decision to have sex? Shouldn't they control the choice to use some means of birth control?

And the last argument—that it is all right to destroy a fetus because it is not quite human yet—has a nasty resonance. Did not the Nazis make the same claim about Jews, gays, and Gypsies?

A UNIVERSAL THEORY

Based on what I know about the predictable and universal process in which organizations are born, grow, age, and die, I believe that a fetus is certainly a human being—because all systems and sub-systems contain, at conception, all the ingredients they will ever possess.

For example, a healthy organizational start-up contains all the ingredients of a grown-up company from its inception. If it didn't, by definition it would not be a healthy start-up. Think of a rosebud: At its "birth," it has all the ingredients of a mature, full-blown rose.

In my experience, this is true of all organic systems. And it goes beyond the physical sub-system—which of course a fetus has—to include the emotional, the intellectual, and the spiritual sub-systems. They are all there in the start-up stage—maybe dormant, but indisputably there. And here is why I believe this to be so:

Is the easy solution necessarily the right solution?

A child does not start her intellectual development from zero when she begins to go to school, right? If that were true, she could not have learned how to speak and understand language. Anyone who spends time with an infant realizes that at birth, she is already actively processing the information her senses give her. In other words, she is learning.

But how do we know for sure *when,* exactly, she began learning? It could have been long before her birth, while she was still in the womb.

The *New York Times Magazine,* in its cover story on May 9, 2010, reported that research has shown that babies can and do distinguish between right and wrong. "You can see glimmers of moral thought … even in the first year of life. Some sense of good and evil seems to be bred in the bone," wrote Paul Bloom, the author of the article and a professor of psychology at Yale.

How do we know that this moral sensitivity appears only after birth? We have very little definite knowledge about the moral and spiritual development of children.

But, if moral and spiritual development were the criteria for deciding who is fully human, most of the earth's population would probably not make the cut.

Maybe we pick on the unborn because they have no one to defend them.

THE MORAL CHOICE

I recognize the need for legal abortion if the mother's or the baby's life is in danger. Or if the pregnancy is the result of a rape. But I would not legalize abortions otherwise. There are other choices available to women besides abortion.

I believe that pregnant women who do not want their babies should receive full medical and emotional support, through the birth of the child and perhaps for a period of time afterward. The baby should be given up for adoption.

Discontinuing a human life is not our right. We did not give it. We have no right to take it.

God gives life, and only God can take it back.

I am against capital punishment for the same reason.

The fact that an option is viable and easy does not make it right.

WHEN MODERATION
WON'T WORK[1]

RECENTLY at a medical convention I attended, the speakers described the benefits of vitamin D3. We get D3 from being exposed to sunlight; thus people who live in the northern regions of the earth often suffer from D3 deficiency. If you are deficient in D3, all kinds of diseases can occur, among them cancer.

But dermatologists also warn *against* exposure to the sun, because of the serious danger of developing skin cancer. Thus, as we increasingly protect ourselves from the sun, more people become deficient in D3.

I recall my mother using an old Sephardic expression in Judeo Ladino, the medieval Spanish language we spoke at home: "*Todu que es demasiadu nu vale*," which means, "All that is exaggerated is no good."

Eating too much of anything, even strawberries, is not good for you. Too much love leads to hate; too much hate is the beginning of madness.

Moderation is the answer. If you love a bit, it is OK to feel some displeasure (I would not say hate) toward someone. Sit in the sun for fifteen minutes in the early morning to get your vitamin D3. But don't sun yourself all day—especially not around noontime—or you will get sunburned and risk developing skin cancer.

Is a little bit of everything really OK? What about a little bit of heroin? A bit of cocaine? Aha! Now we need a new rule: Zero tolerance of whatever takes control of us and enslaves us—whatever causes an addiction. Because when we get addicted, we lose control, and when we lose control we aren't able to follow the rule of moderation.

How about sex? Have you ever known a sex addict? I am not talking about someone with a healthy dose of libido. I am talking about an honest to

---

[1] Adizes Insights, September 2009.

goodness sex addict, who needs to be hospitalized. His sex organs are bleeding from overuse. He is miserable, sick, and desperate.

Too much pleasure, to the point of becoming addicted to it, is no good.

EATING DISORDER

How many of us are addicted to certain foods that are bad for us?

I am one of those. It took me a long time to realize that I am a food addict. I am addicted to bread and cheese. And salami. Salt and oil. Carbs. Processed sugar. If I see it, I eat it. A meal without bread leaves me unfulfilled, anxious: I cannot rest until I find some bread and consume it.

Clearly, I am not in control. I am controlled by something that is stronger than me and plays games with my head, my thoughts. This is typical addictive behavior.

I became obese, on the verge of becoming diabetic. For years, my blood pressure soared, and the pills I took to control my high blood pressure destroyed my kidneys. All because of my addiction.

Have you stopped to think about what *you* are addicted to? Work? Food? Sex? Alcohol? Drugs? Exercise? Tobacco?

Note that what we are addicted to does not feel bad. On the contrary, it gives us pleasure. If it did not, we would not become addicted to it. (How many of us become addicted to okra?) The problem is that, although what we are addicted to gives us pleasure, it is not good for us.

For thousand of years, we could count on the idea that if something was pleasurable, it was probably good for us. If it tasted bad, it *was* bad. That was in the world of scarcity, a much simpler world to live in.

Not true anymore. In a world of abundance, you can have as much pleasure as you want, but *"Todu que es demasiadu nu vale"*—all that is exaggerated is no good. *Too much* is dangerous to your health and happiness.

What is exaggerated in your life? Can you slightly reduce how much or how often you consume it, do it, or use it?

See what happens when you try. If you have difficulty, that means you do not have control. You are addicted. And this addiction can destroy you.

What can you do to get free?

I am at TrueNorth Health Center in Santa Rosa, California, trying very hard to get free of my food addiction. Stay tuned.

ON LOSING WEIGHT[1]

I AM now completing a three-week stay at TrueNorth Health Center in Santa Rosa, California (www.truenorthhealth.com).

Allow me to share with you what I have learned here:

Being overweight is a problem that preoccupies many of us. Numerous articles and books have pointed out that obesity is a contributing factor in serious health problems including diabetes, strokes, and heart attacks, any of which can make the last years of our lives miserable or kill us at an early age.

But the problem of obesity created an opportunity for a multibillion-dollar industry to flourish: the weight-reduction industry. Many bestsellers have been published on the subject, and billions of dollars have been spent on various diet programs, supplements, and even ready-made meals that can be delivered to your home.

The pharmaceutical industry also has benefited enormously from this problem. It has made huge profits manufacturing and selling drugs that suppress appetite and combat diabetes, high blood pressure, and high cholesterol.

What I have learned at this magnificent center is that the solutions these industries offer are based on the wrong diagnosis of the problem—and thus provide the wrong remedies.

RE-DEFINING THE PROBLEM

What is wrong with the diagnosis? What is wrong with the remedies?

Being overweight is *not* the cause of heart attacks. Diabetes, strokes, heart disease, and being overweight are all manifestations of a different problem.

Let me repeat: Being overweight is *not* the cause of high blood pressure or a heart attack. Both being overweight and having high blood pressure are manifestations of a single cause.

---

[1] Adizes Insights, July 2008.

By attacking the weight problem, per se, we are attacking the manifestation, *not* the cause, of these diseases. The probability of having a heart attack will not be reduced. It is like suggesting that a person who is overweight cut off one of her feet. Without that foot, the scale will show that she is the perfect weight. Nevertheless, she is still overweight.

What is the cause of being overweight, of having heart attacks, strokes, and diabetes? Simply stated: We eat the wrong food.

It is not the quantity that is the problem. It is the quality.

Eating less food is not enough for a better and longer life. *Better* food is what we need for a better and longer life.

The Wrong Food

What is wrong with the food we eat?

We eat food that is high in concentrated calories, like sugar and processed carbs. And we eat animal flesh that has a high concentration of protein per pound, plus fat.

Why this preference for concentrated calories and animal protein?

Humans have evolved to naturally prefer food that gives the maximum calories and protein for minimum effort, because for millions of years we lived with a scarcity, not an abundance, of food. Our eating habits developed as a survival mechanism to combat that scarcity.

During scarcity, the more calories and protein we consumed, the more we could store for later on, when no food was available. But today in the developed countries, we live in an era of abundance. During abundance, the *fewer* calories and the *less* protein from animal flesh we consume, the better.

> If you eat healthy food, you will be healthy. It is that simple.

Why do we still eat more than we need, when we can get all the necessary calories simply by consuming food with concentrated calories in very small quantities? Because we are designed by nature to eat as much as our stomachs can hold. Even when we eat concentrated calories and protein, our natural inclination is to keep eating until our stomachs are full—which means we're eating more calories and protein than necessary.

In order to survive, we will have to adapt our diet to a world in which food is abundant, not scarce.

The food industry will not help us. Food-industry companies want to maximize sales, naturally, so they create food that actually increases our appetites by adding fat, sugar, and salt. When we eat sugar-loaded apple pie à la mode, for example, we feel satisfied—for a short while—but then we get hungry again very soon.

The result of eating too much food with highly concentrated calories is that we consume too many calories. When we consume too many calories, the unused calories are stored as fat, which is manifested in being overweight.

Another result of overeating fat and proteins from animal flesh is that we clog our arteries. Furthermore, the large amount of salt added to most processed food causes our blood pressure to rise, which is unhealthy.

The result of eating the wrong food is that we risk obesity, high blood pressure, strokes, and diabetes.

THE WRONG CURE

Some people choose to lose weight by having liposuction—which is the same as cutting off a foot: One of the manifestations of obesity (fat) is taken care of, but if they continue eating protein from animal flesh, which narrows the blood vessels and deposits calcification on the heart, they might die early despite appearing thin.

Others have painful surgery to shorten their intestines. They process their food faster, eat less, and lose weight. They look good. But they have treated the *manifestation* of bad health, not the cause. Unless they change not only *how much* they eat but *what* they eat, they will probably die younger than necessary.

If we want to reduce the chances of having diabetes, heart attacks, or strokes, we should focus on the *cause* of dying prematurely, not the *manifestations* of that cause. We should focus on what makes us *healthy*, not necessarily on what makes us *skinny*.

If the cause of the problem is primarily *what* we eat, and not *when* or *how much*—another fad in the weight-control industry—then that is where our focus should be. Our ultimate goal is to live to our full genetic potential, and not to shorten our lives or make our last years miserable with disease. That means being healthy.

If you eat healthy food, you will be healthy. It is that simple. You will not be overweight, and you will probably not die prematurely.

So why do we focus on weight loss rather than on healthy eating?

This question reminds me of a story:

A man is walking down the street on a very dark night and sees his friend, who is looking for something.

"What are you looking for?" he asks his friend.

"For my keys."

"Where did you lose them?"

"Over there, at the end of the road."

"Then why are you looking here?"

"Because the streetlight is here."

In other words, it is easier to focus on what we can measure, or on taking pills, than to drastically change our eating habits.

You probably know of someone who exercised regularly, took drugs to control her blood pressure and cholesterol, and was at a perfect weight, but had a heart attack and died anyway. What does that tell you? That you can exercise and stay thin by watching your calorie intake, and yet still be dangerously sick in your heart.

To know what better food is, what the right food is, which foods will not cause diabetes, high blood pressure, or high cholesterol—and to lose weight as a *byproduct*, not as the *purpose*, of eating right—you need to come to TrueNorth, or at least read the center-recommended book *The Pleasure Trap*.[2]

Those of you who know Adizes theory will recognize that the TrueNorth philosophy fits perfectly with the Adizes formulas for success.

I am happy to inform you that in one week, my blood pressure went down from 140/100 to 100/80, and my cholesterol went from 170 to 117. And in those six days, I lost six pounds.

I was not hungry. I did not take more or different drugs. If I continue eating the right foods, I expect that soon I will be able to do without any medications.

And I won't be the first one to do so. In the twenty years this center has been in existence, thousands of people have come here and reduced their blood pressure, cleared their arteries, and stopped taking medications.

I wish you the best of health.

---

[2] Douglas Lisle, Ph.D., and Alan Goldhamer, D.C., *The Pleasure Trap: Mastering the Hidden Force that Undermines Health and Happiness* (Summertown, TN: The Book Publishing Co., 2003).

Why 'Let the Consumer Beware' Does Not Work in Practice[1]

BUSINESS organizations, when challenged, defend their questionable practices by saying: "Let the consumer beware."

For example, that is how the tobacco companies defend marketing their cigarettes, which, as we all know, cause cancer not only to those smoking them but also those who inhale them second-hand. The tobacco companies claim to believe that the customer should be able to choose whether to smoke or not. Free country, right?

And how about TV programs that depict violence, casual sex, or vulgar behavior? Consumers are free to change the channel, right?

What about food that can cause obesity, hardening of the arteries, maybe even cancer? Again: Let the consumer decide. People have a choice. Free country. Free choice.

But are we really free to choose?

The free-choice argument assumes that we, the consumers, are in control of our actions, our choices. It assumes that we are free to make our choices.

To be able to choose freely, we must be well informed about what repercussions our choices will have.

It's true that a lot has been done toward informing consumers about the ingredients in their packaged food. There is even a trend in restaurants to tell patrons what goes into the food they are ordering.

Nice.

But this makes the assumption that the data given to consumers is "information." What is the definition of "information"? It is data that is organized in such a way that it can aid decision-making.

---

[1] Adizes Insights, December 2010.

Unfortunately, in reality, most food packaging gives you data, *not* information. For instance, manufacturers can, and do, hide the fact that their product contains lots of sugar by calling it something else. It takes a food engineer or nutrition expert to understand what it says on the package.

But let us give the food companies the benefit of the doubt and assume that their packaging offers us usable information, from which we *can* learn the dangers of consuming the product.

What about TV programs? Is it enough just to warn the viewer about potentially offensive content? Would you call such a warning "data," or is it "information"? To be "information," it needs to remind us of the *repercussions* of watching the program; in other words, what will it do to us? If it does not remind us of the repercussions, it is not effective as a warning. In fact, because what is forbidden tends to attract, the warning could have the opposite effect, tempting us even more strongly to watch the program.

> Mottos such as "Let the customer beware" and "The customer has a choice" are mere fig leaves to disguise strategies that foster addiction.

But, again, even though I doubt it, let us assume we understand the repercussions of the choices we make. Is that all we need in order to be in control of our actions?

I suggest that knowing is not sufficient. We must also have the willpower to act on what we know.

Do we always have that willpower?

I suggest that we do not, because of something called "addiction."

THE 'PLEASURE-PUSHERS'

Many people have an addiction to cigarettes. To alcohol. To violence on TV. (Yes, that's right: addiction to violence.) To sex. To certain foods.

The common denominator to all these addictions is pleasure—and the more pleasure they give, and the faster they give that pleasure, the more addictive they are going to be.

The food industry, alcohol, and TV programming are all "pleasure pushers." They work hard to please us as much and as fast as they can. This is called "good business," because it is extremely profitable. But it also causes us to become addicted.

Mottos such as "Let the customer beware," and "The customer has a choice," are mere fig leaves to disguise strategies that foster addiction. As a result, businesses are able to make profits even if their products cause disease, mental health problems, and sometimes social disintegration.

What to do?

In making social policy, we have a choice: Should we prohibit dysfunctional, addiction-causing products and services (and if we do, then shouldn't we prohibit them across the board, not selectively depending on how powerful a lobby it has); or should we allow market forces to provide those addictive products and services, and let the customer beware?

Both choices have their benefits, but also their costs.

The "freedom to choose" has costs: the current obesity epidemic in the United States; crimes that mimic those on TV programs; deaths caused by drunken drivers.

On the other hand, when Prohibition (of alcohol) was attempted, it did not work. People found ways to produce and consume it despite the law.

Nevertheless, I would still choose prohibition (and, in the case of television, censorship). In my judgment, the price we are paying for our "freedom" is much higher than the price of giving up a phony "freedom" that is rendered useless by addiction anyway.

THE HIGH-TECH ADDICTION[1]

I HAVE already written about food addiction and the addiction to certain feelings. Now I am discovering new addictions. As technology advances to "serve" me, I have become aware that I am increasingly losing control over my life.

There is a Zen story that illuminates this point:

A peasant is walking down the road holding a rope in his hand. At the other end of the rope is a cow.

"Why do you allow the cow to control you?" a passerby asks him.

"It is not controlling me. I am in control," he replies.

"If you are in control, then why don't you let go of the rope?" he is challenged.

What you control also controls you. It is never a one-way street.

The same is true of new technological advances. They make our lives more pleasant, granted, but the more pleasant their contribution, the more dependent on them we become, sometimes to the point of addiction: We can't live without them.

My new addiction is to devices that are supposed to make my life more efficient, and I am not alone in this addiction.

In my consulting practice, I often hold meetings of up to thirty executives, in which I lead a discussion about some problem they are struggling with. I have been doing this for forty years, all over the globe. Over the years, I have noticed a change in behavior: In so-called "developed" countries, it has become increasingly difficult to get the group's undivided attention. Invariably, during the discussion, a large number of people are reading or typing on their BlackBerry devices or laptop computers.

I ask them to stop, and they do; but within minutes they are back to their BlackBerrys (aptly called CrackBerrys by some of their fans/addicts).

---

[1] Adizes Insights, July 2009.

These executives are not the only ones who are literally attached to their BlackBerrys at the hip. My wife will not go with me to a movie unless I leave the BlackBerry at home. More than once, my BlackBerry has vibrated during the movie and, instead of watching the movie, I start reading and answering e-mails.

My clients' spouses tell me that if they ever get divorced, it will be because of the BlackBerry or iPhone. Many people have been known to interrupt a conversation with their spouses—even an urgent discussion—to answer a call or text message.

Sure, it can wait. Sure, it is not so critical; no one's life is in danger. Nevertheless, we just can't leave the vibrating CrackBerry alone. Try to take it away from us and we will steal, lie, and cheat to get it back.

Typical addictive behavior, no?

Beyond the BlackBerry

It is not just the BlackBerry or iPhone anymore. How about Facebook, and Twitter, and blogs? Because there are so many community-building, network-creating devices and sites to keep track of, my productivity is not going up, it is going down. Have you ever calculated how much time you spend on these devices?

Why do we behave like this? Addiction. We are addicted to knowing that someone needs us, wants us, or is there for us.

From the perspective of the (PAEI) code,[2] this seems to me like an (I) addiction, an addiction to affiliating. This (I) addiction is especially potent because humans need to interrelate, to connect. That is why solitary confinement is considered the worst punishment in prison: Without the ability to interrelate, prisoners lose their sense of being human.

This need of ours to relate to other people is being exploited big-time by Internet technology. For instance, my teenage son spends an enormous amount of time in chat rooms. If I try to take away his Internet privileges, he reacts as if I have sentenced him to solitary confinement.

Technology seems to free us. On one hand, these devices do free us from isolation and make communication easier and more pleasant. But on the

---

[2] For more details about the (PAEI) code, see my book *The Ideal Executive: Why You Cannot Be One and What to Do About It* (Santa Barbara, CA: Adizes Institute Publications, 2004).

other hand, they enslave us, because we become dependent on them.

What to do?

The advance of technology cannot and should not be stopped. (The Unabomber tried that, and he is now serving a life sentence in prison.) What is needed is self-discipline.

> *What you control also controls you. It is never a one-way street.*

Who will survive? As with other addictions, success will come to those who have the inner strength to say "No!"

Success is not "out there." It is "in here." And thus, our problems are not "out there" but also "in here." We looked for the enemy, and we found it. And you know as well as I do what it turned out to be.

ADDICTED TO A FEELING[1]

IN one of my lectures, I used the following story to make the point that we should not be disturbed by the conflicts that ensue from disagreements. We should seek what we can learn from a person who disagrees with us. The story is called: "Look for the Pony." Here is the story:

A father had two sons. One was an absolute pessimist. Everything was terrible. Nothing was good enough.

The other was an absolute optimist. Everything was great. Nothing was a problem, etc.

The father decided to do some experiential-style enrichment, to see if he could change his sons' outlooks.

He took the pessimistic kid and put him in a room filled with all the toys a kid his age might desire, just to show him that life is not so bad.

He put the optimistic kid in a room full of horse manure, just to show him that life is not so perfect.

After a while, he went back to see how they were doing.

The pessimist son was sitting in the middle of the room crying his heart out: "Too many toys. I can't decide which one to play with. I am so miserable. Life is terrible."

The optimist son was whistling and singing, and shoving horse manure around. When the father asked him why he was so happy, he replied, "With so much horse s--t, there must be a pony around here."

When someone disagrees with you, ignore the s--t. Ask yourself: Where is the pony? What does he know, or think, or believe, that you do not? Why is he disagreeing with you? What can you learn from the disagreement? (Obviously, if after listening intently you find there is nothing to learn, that it is all s--t and no pony, it's safe to ignore him going forward; he is just wasting your time.)

---

[1] Adizes Insights, September 2009.

But as I was telling this story, I realized that it also had another moral: Both kids *chose* how to feel.

"You are as unhappy as you want to be," according to the famous proverb. We *choose* to be happy or unhappy. How we feel is not caused by something "out there" that causes us to feel one way or another. Happiness has nothing to do with external factors. It is our choosing that matters.

But why would someone choose to feel miserable, unhappy, a victim, and thus age prematurely, and even develop a disease as a result of the depression they feel?

It could be that their unhappiness serves them in one way or another that they are not conscious of. Perhaps that it is how they draw attention to themselves.

> The problem is not that we lack the freedom to choose how we feel, but that we are addicted to feeling bad.

But it could be something else: I suggest it might be an addiction. They are used to the feeling. If they do not feel that way, they will manufacture some illogical reason to feel bad. It may be that they are addicted to a certain chemistry that these feelings generate in the body.

The more I've thought about this, the more I've realized how surrounded we are by sources of addiction: food, work, alcohol, tobacco, and even, for some, exercise. Now I realize that we are addicted to feelings, too. The cues we pick up from our environment are those that enable us to feed our addiction, and we ignore those cues that do not support our addiction.

The problem is not that we lack the freedom to choose how we feel, but that we are addicted to feeling bad.

CHANGING THE CUES

How do you free yourself from a "feeling addiction"?

It is not psychotherapy, I think. Einstein said that the variables that cause a problem are not the variables that will solve the problem. So if the problem is of the head, the solution is in the heart.

In other words, we need to change what the cues mean. We need to make the cue that feeds our addiction feel bad instead of good.

That is what I try to do with my food addiction. I decided that I am sensitive to gluten. Eating bread, which is my addiction, will make me sick. But to be honest, it is not working, because deep inside I know it is not literally true.

Another strategy is to avoid being around food that I am addicted to: If it stays far from my eyes, it will be far from my lips.

But how do you do that with feelings? Take a person who is depressed. He feels normal when depressed, and abnormal when not depressed. So he finds a reason to be depressed, thus feeding his addiction. What now?

Anyone?

PART 3

RELATIONSHIPS

Applying Adizes
to Family Life[1]

I HAVE often been approached at my lectures by people who ask if I have ever written about applying my theories of management and change to personal and family life.

I have not, up to now. I have alluded to it in my writings, but have never actually dedicated a whole article to it. The reason I have not done so is that I do not feel qualified to write about it: I am neither a family therapist nor a psychotherapist. But it has crossed my mind, as I watch how married couples behave and hear about so many divorces (as well as going through a divorce myself many years ago), that there are insights to understanding family dynamics that are discoverable by applying Adizes concepts.

I hope this insight will stimulate debate, rather than be seen as a definitive piece of work. It is not.

THE FAMILY LIFECYCLE

Let us start with the concept of the lifecycle. Everything is subject to change and thus has a lifecycle. Everything is born, grows, ages and dies: people, plants, even stones and stars. Organizations, too, grow, develop, and sometimes die on their own intrinsic and organic lifecycle, from the founding vision and Infancy through the challenges of a young company in the Go-Go stage, to Adolescence to Prime, and beyond that to the aging stages.[2]

People grow in the same way: From infancy, they grow into childhood, adolescence, adulthood, then the stages of aging.

The Adizes methodology begins from a functional point of view. What

---

[1] Adizes Insights, January 2011.

[2] For more information on the theory of lifecycles, see Ichak Adizes, *Managing Corporate Lifecycles* (Santa Barbara, CA: Adizes Institute Publications, 2004).

is the function that is expected—that the entity needs at a particular stage of its lifecycle—and is it being managed in a style that promotes the needed function?

Using that methodology, let us look at the stages of the human lifecycle, first from a male perspective, then a female perspective.

WHAT MEN WANT

So, for example: What does a teenage boy look for in a woman? I suggest that he wants her to be attractive and desired by his peers, which makes him feel like a winner, someone who is sexually desirable himself.

When he starts looking for a bride, however, his requirements change. Now, the question is how good she is at managing a household; how supportive she is of his endeavors; and whether she is gifted as a physical, social, and emotional partner.

When children are born, the expectations change again. How is she as a mother? Can she set boundaries, provide a good example, impart the correct values, and protect the children so they can grow up emotionally, socially, and physically healthy?

When the kids have grown up and are out of the house—when the nest is empty—the functions and expectations change again. Now, a man is looking for a partner for his old age: someone who knows how to use resources efficiently, who is a good traveling companion, and someone with whom he can enjoy both conversation and reading quietly in front of the fireplace.

As the functions needed by the marriage change, so do the expectations. And the behavior, or style, of your partner has to change as well.

WHAT WOMEN WANT

Now let me try to analyze what a woman looks for in a man, and how that, too, changes.

At first, he has to be handsome and healthy, and excel in a field she is interested in, whether it is football, music, or skateboarding. But when she looks for a husband, her needs change: How is he as a provider? How will he be as a father?

When the kids are grown and out of the house, her needs change again: The man she wants to grow old with must be supportive, caring, and interesting, because once the kids are grown, a husband and wife have only each other, so they'd better like and be comfortable with each other.

THE IMPORTANCE OF BEING ADAPTABLE

Now, we know from the Adizes lifecycle theory that a leadership style has to reflect the needs of the organization at its current stage of the lifecycle, and that the style must be adapted as the organization moves into different stages. In the case of family life, at least in developed countries, neither the male nor the female leads the family. Right now, during what might be a transition era, they co-lead. Thus, they should exhibit styles that correspond both to where the family is in its lifecycle and where it is headed next.

At the pre-marriage stage, in order to achieve a healthy lifetime relationship, a man should be looking for a sexy, attractive woman whom he feels would be a good mother. (As a good predictor, he should get to know his prospective mother-in-law.)

When the children are young, she should be a good mother first and above all—while remaining the sexy, attractive woman he married. When the children get older, her style has to reflect the new stage the relationship is entering: She still has to be a good mother, but another priority is how interesting she is to talk to, how good she will be to grow old with.

> Once the kids are grown, a husband and wife have only each other, so they'd better like and be comfortable with each other.

The same holds for what a woman should be looking for in a man. Pre-marriage, she wants a man who is handsome and attractive, but she should also ask herself whether he will be a good provider and a good father. (For an indication, she should get to know her prospective father-in-law.) When the kids are young, she should be looking for a sexy, attractive, physically fit provider who is a good father. When the kids grow older, the physical part is less crucial. More important is how he will be as a partner to grow old with.

I find that when marriages go on the rocks, one reason is that the spouse's style has not changed as the family has moved forward on the lifecycle.

For example, a man may be exclusively looking for a sexy woman, ignoring her potential as a mother (sometimes called the Peter Pan syndrome). Or let's say a woman was a great mother, but now that the nest is empty, she is stuck and does not know how to move into the next stage.

The same holds for males: He is handsome but a terrible provider or a negligent father. He does not change as the needs change.

For a healthy marriage, we need to choose a partner who will be able to change as the family's needs change. Can a woman be attractive throughout the life of her family (and that is a long time), *and* be a good mother, who is *also* a great conversationalist to grow old with? Can a man remain an attractive and physically fit spouse throughout the life of the marriage, *as well as* being a good provider, a great father, and someone you can feel emotionally and socially supported by as you grow old?

As the life span increases, marriages are supposed to last for thirty, forty, and even fifty years. That is a lot of years, during which what is needed from a partner will often change. The question is: Can the partner change? Does he or she have the necessary ingredients to make that change?

CHANGING PARTNERS

I believe that one reason for the trend toward serial marriages, in which people get remarried more than once, is similar to the reason organizations change their leaders: The leadership style is not functional to what the organization currently needs. Take a male, for instance, who is still sexy and attractive many years into the marriage, but still fooling around, trying to score points, and not especially good as a father or provider. He is still a teenager at heart. Right there you have signs of trouble.

Or take another example, of a woman who was a good mother but, when the nest is empty, becomes a bore. She does not know what to do with herself—how to make herself functional to the new reality of her marriage.

So people change partners as their needs change.

I am fully aware that I am oversimplifying these issues. Modern marriages are far too complex to be summed up accurately by the above analysis. Lifecycle theory is only one factor to be highlighted.

COMPLEMENTARY PARENTAL TEAMS

Here is another: A healthy family organization needs a complementary team. Children need both the female and male energies in order to grow up healthy. Thus, we are often attracted to people who are different from us. We fall in love with the person's strengths, which happen to be our own weaknesses. Thus, if one is extraverted, creative, and risk-taking, he or she is often attracted to a potential partner who is more introverted, calm, thoughtful, and risk-averse.

Opposites attract, right? But opposites are also the source of miscommunication and other difficulties.

How such conflicts of style should be handled has been covered in many of my books and lectures. What makes conflict constructive rather than destructive is mutual trust and respect. When there is mutual trust and respect, conflicts that are unavoidable in a marriage, especially where the spouses' styles are very different from each other, become manageable.

When there is no mutual trust and respect, the marriage will eventually dissolve.

Both Sexes Can Be Abusive

Now I have an insight about respect.

I just read in some Mexican newspapers that almost 50 percent of Mexican women believe they have been abused at least once in their marriage.

In many developing countries, physical abuse is not frowned upon; on the contrary, it is expected and sometimes even recommended.

In the developed world, physical abuse still occurs although it is prohibited both culturally and legally. But verbal abuse, such as name-calling or attacking another person's integrity, is much more prevalent. There are no laws that outlaw such abuse, yet it can leave as many psychic scars as physical abuse. And it is just as painful for a man to be verbally abused as for a woman.

PREDICTING DIVORCE[1]

I N my consulting practice, I come across situations where I believe my expertise is too shallow and I need a specialist—for example a psychologist—to help me.

But there have been times when I've brought in a psychologist and found that instead of helping, the psychologist was actually undermining my efforts.

For instance, one executive told me: "I told [the psychologist that] in this company, everyone builds his own army, and we fight a lot. 'Then build your *own* army,' he said."

I was appalled. Here I am trying to build integration, and the psychologist is promoting disintegration.

After some thought, it occurred to me why the psychologist reacted the way he did. A psychologist focuses on the individual—on her mental health and ability to cope and solve her own problems. The assumption is that if the individual is mentally healthy and functioning, the system, comprising multiple such individuals, will function well, too.

Makes sense, no? If the components are no good, why would the system be any good? So, fix the components to fix the system.

But please note that a system is more than the sum of its parts. There are interactions that need to be dealt with.

You can have a situation in which all the parties are mentally healthy and yet the system does not work, as happens in some marriages: The two spouses differ in their expectations of what each of them should be responsible for.

TREAT THE SPOUSE OR THE MARRIAGE?

The psychologist and I developed our therapies out of different assumptions.

The psychologist's focus is on the component, believing that if the

[1] Adizes Insights, December 2009.

components are healthy the system will be healthy. My focus is on the system; I believe that if the system works well, the happiness and behavior of each individual in that system will improve.

Recently I came to the insight that this assumption—that treating an individual will help the system in which this individual interacts—applies to marriage counseling, too.

Assume you have a wife who is very frustrated at not having a career. Being a mom and a wife is not gratifying enough; it does not provide for self-actualization. I find that this phenomenon is very common in modern society. In the past—at least in the traditional Sephardic culture in which I grew up—a wife had a role, a position, and usually a recognized status as a mother.

I remember being invited to dinner at the home of a CEO with a very traditional family. When we rang the bell, the door was opened by the CEO's wife, who stood ready to greet him along with their two small children, who were nicely dressed, their faces washed and their hair combed. She kissed her husband, greeted me, and proceeded to present the kids to her husband, telling him how wonderful they were that day. It reminded me of an executive presenting her achievements to her partner.

I remember my mother. Her undisputed empire was the kitchen, and she took pride in the table she set for her guests and the food she had prepared, sometimes working on it for days. That was her "portfolio," and the guests and family appreciated her labor. "*Bendichas manus*"—"Blessed are the hands who cooked all this"—we told her at every meal. "*Bendichas bokas*" —"Blessed are the mouths that eat it"—she would graciously reply.

One day, soon after I arrived in America, I was invited to a dinner. There was smoked salmon for the main course, and a great cake for dessert. I started to congratulate the lady of the house, telling her how wonderful her cooking and baking were, blessing her hands for preparing it … and then I stopped, because the guest next to me at the table was nudging me in the ribs with his elbow and whispering that I should shut up.

Later, I asked him why he'd stopped me from praising the hostess. "Because she didn't cook any of it. You were embarrassing her. In America we buy it all."

I believe that women have lost the identity and pride that once derived from being a homemaker. Today, status is awarded almost exclusively to those who earn money, and since many wives and mothers do not earn money (on the contrary, they *spend* it), they feel like second-class citizens in the relationship.

INDIVIDUAL THERAPY MAY ENDANGER MARRIAGE

Frustrated, a wife may decide to enter therapy.

And what might happen there?

The therapist will focus on her individual need for self-actualization. "Go out, go find what you want and what makes you happy," the therapist will advise. Soon, the husband will start to notice increasing belligerence from his spouse—to the point that he will fight back by trying to reinforce her role as a wife and mother. Supported by the psychologist, she will stand firm, and in the end it is usually the woman who files for the divorce.

When I meet someone who is divorced or getting divorced, I always ask who pulled the trigger, and invariably the response is that it was the wife. And when I ask, "Was she in therapy?" in most cases the answer is "Yes." (My observations happen to be mostly of well-to-do families.)

If your wife is going to therapy because you are having marital problems, because she is unhappy, because she is resentful of you having a career while her life is static and she feels she is marching in one place, because she resents your claiming extra authority to make financial decisions because you earned the money … get ready. She will start with therapy to deal with her frustrations, and eventually end by asking for a divorce.

Don't let her go alone. Hire a family therapist who focuses on the "system"—the family—rather than on the individual, and go together. Or else your marriage is doomed.

If she goes alone, she may have a better marriage the next time around, because she will be better prepared mentally—but it will be at the expense of your marriage now.

THE MOON AND THE ROLLER COASTER[1]

YEARS ago, a good friend of mine told me that he was unhappy being single. He wanted a change in his life. The dating process, he said, was emotionally exhausting. The women he spent time with were too shallow; he wanted a woman with intellectual depth. He was impatient: Where was she?

Time passed, and lo and behold, my friend tracked down the "right" woman: brilliant, confident, and self-assured. He married her.

A year or so later, my friend told me he was unhappy being married. He wanted a change in his life. His wife—the brilliant woman with intellectual depth—was "too cold." She was also "distant" and "insufficiently intimate."

He got a divorce. A year or so later, he got married to a woman who could "express her love," who was "outgoing" and full of a "zest for life." Six months into the marriage, though, he told me he was, once again, unhappy.

> The goal should not be to find the perfect spouse. The goal should be to find the spouse whose faults you can live with.

His new wife was so needy and made so many demands on his time that he felt suffocated. He wanted a change in his life, and once again he was contemplating divorce.

I remember thinking to myself, "He's looking for a woman who has no faults: the perfect wife."

CHASING THE RAINBOW

If we accept the hypothesis that no one is perfect and entirely free of faults—and this is indeed a hypothesis rather than a fact, and will always remain so, because no one can examine every person on earth or even a scientifically representative sample—then the goal of finding the perfect spouse is unattainable. It's like chasing the rainbow: You may or may not

---

[1] Adizes Insights, June 2010.

enjoy the process, but you're never actually going to catch it. My friend had not yet learned this lesson.

People are like the moon. They have their bright side and their dark side. Which side you encounter depends on how you approach them.

The goal should not be to find the perfect spouse. The goal should be to find the spouse whose faults you can live with.

I believe that God created the experience of "falling in love" so that we would, at least initially, be blind to the faults of the other person.

But it can be a trap. Eventually we wake up, and at that point we cannot help getting to know the other person very well. And then we have to decide whether or not we can live with our partner's faults.

We "fall in love" because of trait A, B, or C that is possessed by the object of our affection. But mature love is something very different. Mature love means to love somebody in spite of faults X, Y, and Z—knowing full well what those faults are and choosing to build our lives around that person anyway.

You do not really know a person until you know both sides of him—both sides of the moon, the bright and the dark side. And then the question is: Do you love the brightness he brings to your life more than you hate the darkness?

Life is a roller coaster with ups and downs that are often totally unexpected. So: When your relations with your partner are down, can you hold your breath until the relationship improves? When relations are up, are you going to be prepared for the inevitable moment when they start to disintegrate?

Expecting the roller coaster to head forever upwards or coast along on a flat plain is a recipe for unhappiness. Expecting, instead, to learn from each up or down shift you experience together is a much more realistic, and fulfilling, goal for mature relationships.

What is true about relationships, of course, is true in the larger sense about all of life. Life lived well is going for the roller-coaster ride without fear, in the hopeful expectation that every down will have its corresponding up, and learning from each new change that life presents.

HOW TO DO BUSINESS
WITH FRIENDS AND FAMILY[1]

I RECENTLY learned that in the Serbian traditional culture, a brother is forbidden to lend money to his brethren.

In the Jewish tradition, similarly, lending money to a friend or family member is not recommended. Instead, you should *give* them, as a gift, as much money as you can afford, even if it is less than they need.

What is going on? And why are family businesses chock full of intrigue, fights, and hard feelings, sometimes even leading to tragedies?

I finally understood why when I got involved in business endeavors with my brother-in-law, and experienced personally what happens when those Serbian or Jewish cultural recommendations are ignored.

Why should you avoid lending money to family or friends, and instead give them as big a present as you can afford? Because when you give a gift, you let go of your expectations for prompt repayment.

On the other hand, when you lend money, you end up looking over the shoulder of the person you loaned money to. If he spends money on anything beyond absolute necessities, you will find that you resent it and hold it against him, and will continue resenting him for having a normal life until he pays back what he owes you.

And this resentment is a two-way street, not a one-way street. The recipient of your loan will resent you, too, for his dependence on you. "Dependency breeds contempt," a psychiatrist friend once told me. There is also a Chinese expression: "Why do you resent me so much? I did not help you!"

If you lend your sister money and she does not pay you back for some reason, you will resent it, she will resent you, and the relationship will suffer.

In the Jewish tradition, a righteous person gives *tzedakah*, an anonymous

[1] Adizes Insights, October 2009.

donation. He does not expect anything back, and the recipient does not know whom to resent … so anonymous gift-giving is beneficial for both benefactor and recipient.

Why are family partnerships usually messier than non-family businesses? Because when you start to negotiate with family, you rarely think the details through to the end. Nor do you maintain arms-length relations, or construct agreements approved by your lawyers, as you would with a non-family member.

When going into business with a brother or sister or cousin, you just assume, "We'll work out whatever problems arise, because we are family." Nothing is nailed down, and necessary details are left out.

> *"Dependency breeds contempt," a psychiatrist friend once told me.*

As we all know, the Devil is in the details. And when the Devil does eventually appear, there is no more vicious fight than one between brothers and sisters; it can be a struggle to the death.

The closer you are to the person you are negotiating with, the more careful you have to be, even though it feels uncomfortable to negotiate and argue with family. But what we don't do when we begin the journey, we will *have* to do when we get stuck somewhere along the way. And by then, it may be too late to negotiate. We may find ourselves fighting with family and possibly destroying it.

There is no free lunch. Particularly where family is concerned, it is best to anticipate the divorce before you get married.

NOTE

I have been asked why I recently started using my middle name, Kalderon, in my signature.

It is my mother's maiden name. Everyone on that side of my family perished in Treblinka, and there is no one left to carry on the name, which originated in Spain hundreds of years ago.

In 1492, the Inquisitors expelled my family from Spain because they refused to abandon the Jewish religion. I feel a deep need to keep my mother's family name alive.

THE UNWANTED BYPRODUCT
OF BEING CREATIVE[1]

LET me start with the bottom line: My insight is that creative people often have problems with intimacy.

Why?

When I create, rather than just being creative—when I write or do coaching or consulting—I am one hundred percent present, focused on what I do. If you stop me in the middle of my writing or consulting and ask me which day it is or even what season we are in, it will probably take me thirty seconds to disengage my mind from my work enough to be able to answer.

When I create, I am not in the room. I am actually nowhere. So I do not notice or feel anybody else around me.

What happens when I am not busy creating? I am still creative as a person; thus, my mind often wanders. My body is there but my mind is not where my body is. I think about something or observe something intently. My son or wife could be talking, but, triggered by something they said, my mind starts to wander, and then I am listening to my mind, not to what they are saying.

> Intimacy requires that your mind be present and focused on the other person.

It's hardly strange that they claim I am the worst of listeners.

I am now on a two-week vacation in Paris with my fifteen-year-old son. He is not getting younger: This is probably my last opportunity to bond with him.

But I am having a hell of a time being present. And I know that if my mind is not where my body is, I will have no lasting memories of being with him. So I am continually struggling to bring my mind to the place I am in physically; to bring my mind to where *he* is, instead of somewhere else.

---

[1] Adizes Insights, June 2009.

I don't believe this happens only to me; I think all creative people whose minds are busy all the time have problems being intimate. After all, intimacy requires that your mind be present and focused on the other person.

Is there any research on the subject that anyone is aware of? What are the methodologies for staying present when the mind is wandering? I know about meditation, but what about the day-to-day just being with someone?

I would appreciate your input.

SIGNS OF DISINTEGRATION[1]

O N one hand, it's hard not to notice that the world is becoming "smaller." The Internet is one cause; others include air travel; a reduction in visa requirements; the rise of multinational corporations, especially in the hospitality industry (and they all serve the same American breakfast); American music piped in everywhere, all over the globe; the same cars; the same international coverage by the media. ...

As I travel around the world, I no longer feel the differences I used to expect when I crossed national boundaries. More and more, it seems like we are all living in the same global village—maybe even the same city.

These signs can be interpreted as signs of global integration. But sameness does not mean integration. It just means sameness.

On the other hand, I definitely see signs of *dis*integration.

We know that integration is a function of mutual trust and respect. When MT&R decline, integration, too, declines.

The following are some signs of declining trust:

AIDS has undermined trust enormously, and for good reason. Someone who is carrying the virus might not even know it, because he may not have symptoms until years after he has been exposed. It is reasonable to wonder how many partners he's had during those years. And it's just as reasonable for the person you are wondering about to wonder the same thing about you.

> *Sameness does not mean integration. It just means sameness.*

Can you trust a "sexual chain" when it appears to show that no one was infected?

No!

Thus, safe sex is now a requirement. And every use of a condom manifests a lack of trust.

---

[1] Adizes Insights, January 2011.

Condoms are also recommended to avoid unwanted pregnancies, and that, too, can be a manifestation of no trust: The partners do not trust each other to take precautions like the pill.

Here is another: Remember the fear of SARS? I travel on airplanes a lot. If someone on the plane started coughing, I could see the people near him getting scared. Should they breathe the air near him?

I love folk dancing. In Israel recently, I watched for an hour as people performed circle dances on the Tel Aviv promenade. Circle dancing used to involve holding hands. Now, people still dance in a circle, but each dancer by himself.

The same thing has happened to ballroom dancing. Compare the waltz, the tango, the rumba—to disco dancing. No one touches anymore.

What about the phenomenon of pre-nuptial agreements? Recently, I also read about a new type of insurance policy: divorce insurance. How is *that* for mutual trust? Now, when we get married we need a legal agreement as to who will own what if we get divorced. And, to minimize losses, both bride and groom (and maybe the mother-in-law, too) buy a divorce insurance policy.

SHRINKING WHILE SIMULTANEOUSLY GROWING

At the same time that the world seems to be growing smaller, it also gets bigger. Children move further away; my children, for instance, are all over the United States. How often do I see my children and grandchildren? Not very often, compared to the time of our grandparents. Back then, travel was more difficult, but families stayed closer together.

Television has contributed to the disintegration, too. Yes, you can watch CNN and know what is happening in the world, but television has also caused people to stay at home more, watching TV instead of getting together in person.

E-mail, Skype, Facebook—all the so-called community building software—has enabled more interacting, but less *relating*.

To be honest, I prefer the way life used to be: It was simpler, time moved more slowly, and friendships were deeper and more real.

In effect, our standard of living has gone up, but our quality of life is down.

WHAT IS LIFE ABOUT?[1]

I REMEMBER sitting next to my mother's hospital bed during the days just before she died. She was not conscious, to the best of my knowledge. Her eyes were open, but they were glassy, with no expression in them.

Still, there was an effort there. Or that is what I thought. An effort to see, to hold on.

I tried to imagine what she was feeling during those last moments on earth: trying to see; trying to have just one more second with someone she loved (in her case, me). What would she have given for one more second to see me, to hold onto me? *Just one more second.*

I found myself wondering: If *I* were dying, what would *I* give to hold onto life and see the people I love next to me—for just one more second?

Whom would I want next to my bed in my last minutes of life? And whom would I want to *leave*, to free space for the people I love and to avoid wasting those precious last moments?

Then I thought: Why do I have to wait until I'm dying to free my life from those I do not love and who do not love me?

After all, I am dying already: If life is a fixed number of breaths, for every breath I take there is one less in my future. So why wait until my last breaths to surround myself only with those I love and who love me? Why am I wasting my life trying to make relationships work when there is no love?

DO WHAT YOU LOVE

I realized that almost everything I do, including writing this blog, is for love. If I did not love writing, why would I do it? For fame, for potential money? That would be wasting my life, would it not?

All my consulting work is for love. If I did not love helping organizations, why would I do it?

---

[1] Adizes Insights, April 2010.

I am a good speaker. You know why? Because I honestly and truly love my audience. Someone once told me that when I lecture it feels as if I am making love to the audience. Hmmm. ...

But not everything in my life is done out of love. Some of what I do is to earn a living. A lot of it is to accommodate, to appease, to avoid pain, to make others happy even though it makes me unhappy.

I have to keep reminding myself of my insight in my mother's hospital room. Would she have spent *her* last seconds of life trying to accommodate someone, or would she have spent those last seconds loving and being loved?

I have resolved to review whom I spend time with, whom I dedicate my time to—what I do and why.

I just gave a keynote presentation to over 5,000 physicians who specialize in "anti-aging"—prolonging healthy life. The message I gave them is that *love* prolongs life. Just look at people who are in love: They look radiant, youthful—while people who hate look old.

LOVE PROLONGS LIFE

My mother died when I left her bedside to get something to eat. Since then, I have asked many people whose loved ones died in a hospital whether anyone was in the room when they died. And invariably I have heard that death occurred when there was no one in the room.

Yes, of course. Because love prolongs life.

How much love is there in *your* life? Whom will you want near you as you are breathing your last breaths?

Whom would you *not* want?

Why don't you get rid of them now?

I have noticed that successful companies have lots of love in them: They love their clients; management loves their employees and vice versa; the organization loves the community it is in and takes care of that community.

Loves prolongs not only our own lives, but the lives of the organizations we work in or with; the lives of the communities we live in; and the countries we belong to.

I like Mahatma Gandhi's philosophy: "Live as if you will die tomorrow; learn as if you will live forever."

PART 4

PROBLEM-SOLVING

MANAGING CHANGE,
IN BUSINESS AND IN LIFE[1]

D EAN Purg, professors, alumni, graduating class, and friends:
This presentation—"Managing Change, in Business and in Life"—
has four components: change, management, life, and business. Let us address
each concept separately and analyze how they might relate to each other.

CHANGE

Change has been here forever and will continue to be with us in the
future. What is new, however, is that change is accelerating. Humanity has
made more technological innovations in the last hundred years than in
the whole history of humanity. There are more scientists living today than
cumulatively since the dawn of mankind.

Faced with more frequent change, we have to make strategic decisions
more often than our forefathers. Our grandfathers probably made one major
strategic decision in their entire lifetimes, and our parents made only a few.
But we—I mean my generation —are making major strategic decisions every
ten years or so; and you, the graduating class, may find yourselves making
major critical decisions—decisions that will cause serious changes in your
personal lives or in the organizations you will be managing—every two or
three years. In fact, one strategic decision may not even have been fully
implemented yet, or had time to bring results, before you will be pressured
into making new strategic decisions anyway.

And there is something else that is new: Change is becoming increasingly
systemic. A change in a market must be addressed promptly by supply chain
management, which can have an impact on finance as well as on the human

[1] Acceptance speech for honorary doctorate, December 7, 2007, at commencement ceremony, IEDC,
School of Management, Bled-Slovenia; published in Adizes Insights, December 2007.

resources needed to address those market changes. It's no longer possible to successfully solve a problem caused by systemic change by addressing only one organizational sub-system. If you attempt to do so, the organization will almost certainly suffer debilitating side effects.

We must also keep in mind that the world is becoming increasingly interlinked. A problem that emerges in one country can resonate and migrate throughout the world.

This means that while the whole system is spinning faster and faster, and the world's interdependencies are growing "tighter and tighter," and the time span within which we must deal with these interdependencies is growing shorter and shorter.

The repercussions are easy to predict: accentuated and accelerated S-T-R-E-S-S.

Thus, it is becoming increasingly important to learn how to *manage* change efficiently and effectively—and that brings us to the next concept in this presentation:

MANAGEMENT

What does it mean to manage?

To manage means to make the right decisions and implement them efficiently.

But as I said before, making the right decisions is more difficult now than in the past—and it is going to become even more complex in the future. And the difficulties do not stop there. Implementing those decisions, regardless of how wise they are, is also going to become more difficult.

Why? Because the labor force no longer consists of ordinary blue-collar workers—people who simply take orders, carry them out, and are just happy to have a salary to take home. The new labor force is increasingly well educated. We don't employ "hands" anymore. We are looking for brains.

But the trouble with brains is that they think independently; they do not simply follow orders. Members of this new labor force want to participate in decision-making: to have some control over their working lives, to make an impact, to have a choice.

This means that the managerial process will become increasingly democratized. And the repercussions of this democratization are also predictable: It will be more difficult to implement change. Democracy, after all, is based on the legitimacy of dissension, and dissension rarely simplifies the implementation of changes. Thus, it should surprise no one that CEOs' most common complaint is that their decisions do not get implemented quickly enough—or at all.

So, my dear graduating class, I am glad I am not in your shoes. What you are going to face is much more complex and difficult than what I had to face when I graduated. You have a much more difficult time ahead of you. You will have to make the right decisions; make them quickly and correctly; and implement them impeccably in this new participative environment, where many people have both the right and the inclination to resist your decisions—while at the same time, critical new problems will be thrown at you, nonstop, at an accelerated pace.

Phew!

What advice can I, with more experience (simply because I have lived longer), offer to you?

Let us review from the beginning: Because change is accelerating, you will have to make more decisions and make them faster; and in order to implement them promptly, you will have to be politically astute enough to deal with your company's internal politics without shooting yourself in the foot.

This spells *S-T-R-E-S-S* in capital letters. And all these changes and stresses can affect your personal life.

Which brings us to the next item in the title of this presentation:

LIFE

You will find that you have less and less time available for your family—and even worse, less and less time for yourself.

What I personally have found out is that it is difficult, if not impossible, to *find* time for your family and for yourself. It is natural to say: "As soon as I finish this project, I will have time for my family," or for yourself. But it doesn't work that way. Even before you finish one project, the next one is waiting for you, because the first one creates the conditions in which the second one will emerge.

So, time for family and self cannot be *found*. You have to *take* the time. Regard this time just as you would a religious holiday. God did not say: "When you find the time, celebrate Christmas or Hanukah," or whatever your religious holiday happens to be. The religious manuals—regardless of whether we are speaking of the Old Testament, the New Testament, or the Koran—simply state that on such and such a date you must stop working and celebrate your religious holiday. Period. And the same goes for the Sabbath, whether it is on Friday, Saturday, or Sunday. You do not take the seventh day off only when you happen to find the time and are free—because *that never happens*. Work always creates more work. It never, ever ends. You must take rest when the seventh day arrives. Period.

If you look at religious people, you will find that they are generally less stressed. They have a manual: their holy book, whichever one it is. Their religion tells them what to do and what not to do. And they have faith. They surrender to a higher consciousness and let that consciousness decide some of the complexities. They trust that God knows what S/He is doing.

But what about those who are not religious? What are *they* supposed to do?

The nonreligious have, perhaps, the more difficult job. They have to develop their *own* manual to guide their behavior. They have to learn how to consciously *take* time off, to stop work and rest. They have to consciously, all by themselves, develop that discipline, rather than just following the manual that was given to them.

What will happen if you *do* slow down and consciously take time off? Will it mean that others, who do not slow down and who do not take the time to integrate themselves, will pass you by? Will the problems you haven't yet dealt with grow worse? Will these breaks you take eventually destroy you?

These fears are perfectly normal. Let me suggest how you can deal with them.

Building a company, or a career, is like mining for gold. If you just keep digging without taking the time to build an infrastructure, someday the mine may collapse on you and you will find yourself trapped.

You need to build, then stop and integrate what you have built, and then reorganize so that you can find the energy to drive on to the next level. And you need to repeat this process for as long as you live.

Years ago I was with a client, scheduling our next meetings. I suggested a certain date in March. He replied, "Oh, no, sorry, I cannot do it on that day. I will be on my honeymoon."

I was shocked. I had had dinner with him and his wife only the night before. How had he managed to get divorced and remarried overnight?

Seeing my bewilderment, he explained, "My wife and I have a honeymoon every year on the anniversary of our wedding day. And we have done so for the last twenty-five years, because *one honeymoon is not enough for a lifetime of marriage.*"

Do you see the wisdom in that? Take time off. Take that time—or you will find that change will suck you in. It will present more and more challenges that will be increasingly attractive and hard to decline—and while your career is going stratospheric, your health (mental as well as physical) is going to deteriorate, and ultimately you will find that not

> *Time for family and self cannot be found. You have to take the time.*

only do you not know your children and your spouse, you will not know *yourself,* either. You will not recognize yourself or who you have become.

Change causes disintegration, and disintegration is the root of all diseases. Change will drive you. Change will present opportunities that will make you successful, as measured by one set of criteria, but also be the source of your failures, as measured by another set of criteria. To deal successfully with change, we need to practice conscious management. Conscious management means being aware of what is happening—and to *consciously, intentionally,* plan and schedule time for integration as a counterforce to the disintegration caused by change.

Now, what should you do during the time you take off from your busy schedule? Sit and contemplate your navel?

I once had a client who told me he'd lost all his net worth in the real estate crash of the 1980s. Nevertheless, he looked healthy and in good spirits. So I asked him what his secret was, and he told me something I would like to share with you.

He said our biggest assets are our health, our families, and our good friends. As long as we hold onto those three blessings, money can come and go. If you lose your health, nothing else seems very important anymore. If you lose your family, it is like a death. Good friends will always help you find a way out of a crisis, whatever it is.

But these three assets do not accumulate by themselves. You have to invest in them to make them grow. Many of us take them for granted—until we lose them.

Ironically, many of us don't appreciate the most valuable elements of our lives until they're gone. You do not understand the value of health until you are sick. You do not value democracy until you've lived in a dictatorship. You don't sufficiently treasure a supportive, loving family until, God forbid, you lose it. And you never realize the importance of having friends until the day comes when you need them—and you have none.

So, the higher the rate of change, the more problems you will have, which means you'll have less and less time to take care of your health, your family, and your friends. You might be busy building one asset, the material one, while meanwhile losing the most important assets there are.

To build those important assets—health, family, and friends—you must consciously *take* the time, schedule it and treat it as if it were a part of your religious tradition. Why? Because if you wait to *find* the time, the ever-accelerating rate of change will ensure that you will never find it.

I want to add something to what I just said—something that goes beyond personal health, family, and friends.

The institution of business, in comparison to not-for-profit organizations, has been developing for hundreds if not thousands of years, and by now it is a well-oiled machine. It has capital markets. It has human resources—you, for example—who are trained to manage and to lead. It has well-developed procedures, theories, and practices. It has measurable goals, and it rewards performance. It is so effective and efficient that it is actually working *too* well: It is destroying our environment, the world we live in, the world we are going to leave to our children and grandchildren.

Individually, people are worried, but the responsibility to solve the problem cannot be left to governments; they are too slow to act, and when they *do* act, they tend to bureaucratize everything. The NGOs cannot do it, either. Compared to the business community, NGOs are still in the Stone Age of their development: They do not have capital markets; they fight among themselves for limited philanthropic resources; and they rely to a large degree on volunteers, who are not as abundant nor as reliable as paid employees.

It is as if we are living on a motorboat that has one enormous and roaring engine, while its second engine is weak and continually stalls. It is not difficult to predict what is going to happen—where this boat called Earth is heading. I believe we are advancing toward a disaster of fatal dimensions. We are literally destroying our planet. I have on my desk a sign that says: "If you do not take care of your body, where are you going to live?" By the same token: If we do not take care of our planet, where are we going to live?

Since there is, so far at least, no global institution that can prevent this universal disaster, the only answer is that each of us must take personal responsibility for what he or she does.

That brings me to the fourth and last topic of this presentation:

BUSINESS

What is the role of business in society? Some business schools do teach social responsibility—in other words, that business should take on a social role as well as an economic role.

Both F.A. Hayek,[2] in the 1940s, and Nobel Prize-winning economist Milton Friedman, in the 1960s,[3] made the opposite argument: The role of business is business. Businessmen have to be responsible to their investors. Guarding the welfare of society is the job of other institutions.

But let me reiterate: There *are* no existing institutions that can stop the impending disaster—none that are as effective as the institution of business that is driving this runaway train.

What to do?

Doctors, in their medical training, learn as one of their first principles to "First, do no harm."[4] And that is what you, the future leaders of business, should do when you graduate, too: pledge with all your heart to *"Do no harm."* Represent the owners and give them the return on their investment. Do that, with all your passion. But at the same time, make sure you do not incur a cost that future generations will have to pay. *Do no harm.* Do not destroy the environment, the society, the world we live in. We have no other world to leave to our children. *Your* children.

Do not destroy the world on one hand and then donate money to charity to show how socially responsible you are. *Just do no harm.*

Be conscious of your deeds, and take responsibility for what you do to yourself, to your family, and to the world we live in and owe so much to.

Thank you.

---

[2] F.A. Hayek, *The Road to Serfdom* (Chicago: Univeristy of Chicago Press, 50th anniversary edition, 1994).

[3] Milton Friedman, *Capitalism and Freedom* (University of Chicago Press, 1962).

[4] Contrary to popular belief, the phrase "First, do no harm" does not appear in the Hippocratic Oath (which does, however, counsel doctors to "refrain from doing harm"). Hippocrates may have coined the more famous phrase in the first book of his treatise, *Of the Epidemics.*

How Not to Decide[1]

I MAGINE that you are walking down an unfamiliar street and come to an intersection. Now you must make a decision: Go left? Right? Forward? Or should you turn around and go back?

Some people have enormous difficulty making decisions when high uncertainty and risk are involved. When they reach that intersection and cannot figure out which way to go, they decide *not* to decide. At least, they *believe* they have not decided. In reality, by default, they *have* decided—to stay where they are.

Sometimes, of course, it makes sense to postpone making a choice while you wait for more information. If you believe the cost of waiting is lower than the value of the information you are waiting to receive, then that is a wise course of action.

But it is dangerous to postpone a decision for long—because if you wait long enough, the situation that has been frozen in place will have become the new reality—a sort of continuous temporary, otherwise known as permanent.

Practice Conscious Management

Take me, for instance. I did not immigrate to the United States; I just went there to study. Then, after graduation, I decided to stay on temporarily, to earn some money and publish some articles before returning "home." One day at a time, that temporary decision prolonged itself into a forty-seven-year stay.

To this day I have never actually decided to stay. But here I am anyway, forty-seven years later.

Here is another example from personal life: You might be a non-smoker who one day makes an impulsive decision to smoke just one cigarette, just to try it out. You do not decide to start smoking. But after one cigarette, you

---
[1] Adizes Insights, April 2010.

light a second and a third—and before you know it, you are hooked. Now you are a smoker—even though you never actually chose to become one.

Every action we take, whether we consciously decide to take that action or not, becomes a decision by default, if it is repeated often enough or for long enough. Repeat a behavior, and it becomes a habit. Habit is the form; behavior is the function.

Here is another example: In the beginning, the flow of a river creates the riverbank: Function creates the form. Eventually, that riverbank will determine how the river flows: The form now impacts the function.

> Repeat a behavior, and it becomes a habit. Habit is the form; behavior is the function.

Why all this philosophizing? Because it is important to practice what I call "conscious management": Are you conscious, not just of the decisions you make and what is happening between your ears, but also of the actions you take without actually deciding? Are you sure that your actions (or non-actions) do not become your decisions by default?

It is OK to decide not to decide; just be sure that your "holding" actions don't add up to a decision you would never consciously have chosen.

WHAT IS A COMMITMENT?
APPLYING BUSINESS LOGIC
TO PERSONAL LIFE[1]

WHAT would you think if someone told you that a certain CEO was angry at the company's largest competitor and repeatedly demanded that the *competition* had to change its behavior?

You would think the guy was out of his mind.

How about if I told you that there was a CEO whose company was losing sales, whose solution was that the *clients* had to change their behavior and start buying his products?

You would laugh at me, would you not?

But isn't that what we do in personal life? When we have a problem with a colleague at work or with a neighbor, we say: "She has to change!" When we have a problem with our spouse, we absolutely insist that the spouse has to change.

Except that we already know from experience that this does not work.

WHO HAS TO CHANGE?

The competition is not going to change because of us. Neither will the clients. They change for reasons of their own. We can provide those reasons— but that means *we* have to act; *we* have to change *first*.

This focus on who has to change is one of the building blocks of the Adizes methodology. When we diagnose a company, in listing its problems, we insist that the problem be phrased in such a way that the problem is clearly controllable by the company. Thus, instead of saying that we have a problem with "unpredictable interest rates" (this was once listed by a bank client), we

---

[1] Adizes Insights, June–July 2005.

should say: "*We* do not have a strategy to deal with unpredictable interest rates." Instead of saying: "increasing competition," say: "*We* do not have an effective strategy to stop the increased competition."

How Do You Measure Commitment?

While there can be commitment with no change (in other words, we are committed that *others*—not ourselves—should change), there can be no change without commitment. There will be no implementation of strategy, no matter how good or necessary it is; no new direction that is followed; no real action.

But how should you measure commitment?

The following insight was given to me by my associate Carlos Val de Susso of Brazil.

What would you think of a business person who told you that she was committed to opening up the New York market, but who did not allocate any time and financial resources to make it happen?

> There is no commitment without a cost. The more you are willing to "pay," the more committed you are.

You would call her a dreamer.

What would you think about a person who was willing to die in order to advance a particular political or religious idea or belief?

You would consider this person extremely committed.

Now, what does this tell you?

There is no commitment without a cost. The more you are willing to "pay," the more committed you are. If a person is willing to enter the New York market with a $10 million investment—but that is only a miniscule part of her total resources—while someone else makes an investment of $50,000—which is everything she has—obviously you would say that the latter is more committed.

What does that tell you? The bigger the *sacrifice* that's offered, the bigger the *commitment*.

A sacrifice is not only measured in money. It could be time that must be sacrificed for the cause, or pain that must be endured to fight those who oppose the change—because what you are committed to is making a *change*, which means you have to let go of one thing to get something else. There is no free lunch. You have to invest time, money, and energy, which are all manifestations of commitment, to make the change happen—whether it is entering the New York market or starting a revolution.

Even if you say, "Although there is change around me and pressure to change, I am committed to staying the course and *not* changing," you will probably have to make some sacrifices. Holding to one's position or course of action and resisting pressures to change also requires energy and often involves taking risks. Thus, that too is a commitment that involves a cost.

COMMITMENT WITHOUT SACRIFICE?

Is it possible to effect change without paying the price, without making a sacrifice? I have noticed, and even personally experienced, commitments made without the willingness, or readiness, to pay the price. For example, you make the commitment to exercise, but without actually allocating time away from something else in order to do it; or the commitment to control your anger, without the willingness to pay the price of swallowing your pride and shutting up.

> Despite the slogan "All you need is love," love is not enough.

Another example: People often say, "I am committed to going on a diet"—but as soon as they feel hungry, their commitment evaporates. They are not willing to pay the necessary price to lose weight, to make change happen. They are not truly committed. They will never lose weight on their own.

What do you mean to say when you declare, "I am committed to my marriage"? What it *should* mean is that although there are challenges to the institution of marriage, although there are temptations, you are willing to resist them and stay the course of marital fidelity; you are willing to pay the price of saying "no" to "opportunities." You are willing to endure the pain that some conflicts, which happen in every marriage, bring.

In today's free-for-all society, staying married requires commitment: Despite the slogan "All you need is love," love is not enough. Commitment involves emotional and time investments that, in the hectic world we live in, some might not want to make. Some people want to change from single life to married life without paying for that change. It is like wanting to change from being a local company to a national or global company without any investment.

We know it does not work.

It is not strange that the higher the rate of change, the higher the rate of divorce, or that people are waiting longer and longer to get married. We live in a society of instant gratification, minimizing sacrifices. As change accelerates and the need for commitment increases (thus increasing the sacrifices), there is more and more temptation to call it quits and go back to single life, or to postpone marriage as long as possible.

The greater the change that is affecting us or that we want to implement, the higher the commitment and the price we must be willing to pay.

Whenever there is change, which requires a different course of action, ask yourself these questions:

Who has to change? (And start with *yourself*.)

How *big* is the change?

Does the commitment reflect the magnitude of the change required?

Does the price you are willing to pay reflect the magnitude of the change that you want to make? Are you launching big ships in shallow waters, or is the water deep enough?

WHAT WENT WRONG?[1]

F ROM time to time, everyone in life makes what we call a "mistake." This is a situation where what was expected either did not happen, or it happened with some unanticipated collateral damage.

How should one analyze a "mistake"? How should we go about answering the inevitable question: "What went wrong?"

It is in the nature of being human that we require an explanation for "mistakes." Usually, we cannot rest until we have identified some cause. When none is readily available, we may suddenly become religious: "It's God's will." "The Devil made me do it." "It was not meant to be." And so on.

Those "religious" attributions are attractive because they are simple and easy to use. The only problem is that they do not allow us to learn from our mistakes!

Another easy-to-use attribution of causality is to personalize the cause. This process is known by many names, but is most memorably known as a "witch-hunt." Like the seemingly religious attributions, they are easy. You just "put a bell around someone's neck": In other words, you track down the "troublemaker," the person "responsible," and make sure he is easy to recognize from a distance—just like a cow with a bell. Notice that the "troublemaker" is objectified and dehumanized in this example.

Concluding that a specific person is culpable generally does not lead to anyone learning from the "mistake," either—unless a) the problem is in fact this person's fault, which is not always the case; or b) the person who is supposed to learn can do so even though he or she has been objectified, which is even rarer.

How then is one to learn from "mistakes," so that they will not be repeated?

First, we must realize that every conscious action has two components:

---

[1] Adizes Insights, July 2010.

the making of the decision, and the implementation of the decision. This leads to an important question sequence: Was the decision wrong? Or was the decision right, and the implementation poor?

MOVING BEYOND JUDGMENT

Let's begin with the first question in the sequence. What can be learned if the decision itself was wrong?

To make any headway here, we must move beyond simply being judgmental: "The good decision should have been...." We do not learn from judging. We learn by analyzing the process by which the wrong decision was made, so that, the next time around, we can follow a better process. Were the right people involved in making the decision? How did they go about deciding? Was there a constructive exchange of ideas before the decision was finalized? Was all the pertinent information considered? Were both the pros and cons of any alternative decision correctly valued?

The questions you just read are only a representative sample of the questions we must use to analyze the process by which the decision was made, but they will serve to give you a sense of this kind of analysis.

Now let's move on to the second question in the sequence. Let's assume the decision was appropriate, and it is the implementation that needs reviewing. In this case, we should consider a different set of issues if we are to analyze and learn from the mistake. For instance: Which member of the team, if any, did not do what he or she was supposed to do? Why not? Was the timing off? Was the intensity of the task of implementation simply too high for the people responsible? Or, conversely, was the task perceived as too easy, and thus overlooked or minimized in importance?

It is imperative, in my view, to differentiate between errors in decision-making and errors in implementation. They have totally different causes, and yield different lessons.

But what lesson can be learned if the analysis shows that the decision was done well and the implementation was impeccable?

We learn humility: that we are not in control of all of the variables that affect our lives. In spite of doing our best, not everything works the way we want it to work. In this case, we must learn to accept our limitations and to surrender our ego—a lesson that, it seems, must be learned again and again throughout our lives.

What Can We Learn
from Dion?[1]

DION Friedland is a South African businessman who resides in Miami
and London.

Thirty-some years ago, Dion was a client. Ever since then, he has been
a close friend. I have been with him while he negotiates, when he deals with
employees, and when he spends time with his family. I have been watching
him from up close, and there is much to learn from him.

Dion is a very successful businessman. He started a retail store chain in
South Africa, moved to the United States to build a sales training firm, then
opened a store chain to sell lighting fixtures. Next, he became an art dealer
and then established a fund comprised of other funds, which manages money
invested in hedge funds. He also has a company that owns the patent on a
process that converts water into disinfectants or detergents without using
chemical additives.

While accomplishing all of this, he also built, owned, and sold one of the
top ten resort hotels in the world, located in the Caribbean.

By and large, most of his endeavors have succeeded. How did he do it?

One thing I've noticed over all these years is that I have never, *ever* seen
Dion angry; upset for a few seconds, yes, but never angry, despite many
situations that might have warranted it. He solves problems without betraying
any emotion.

The guy simply has no "internal marketing"—no internal conflict.
Internal marketing leads to symptoms of paralysis, inconsistent decision-
making, the reversal of decisions already made—and usually causes great
anguish and loss of energy. Dion exhibits none of that; he decides and then
he executes.

---

[1] Adizes Insights, August 2010.

That's another thing: I have never seen him fail to implement a decision.

Simply stated, Dion has the strongest self-discipline of anyone I have ever encountered.

Many of us decide, but then waver when it comes to implementation. With Dion, implementation is prompt and swift and reflects exactly the decision taken. Here is an example: He is now 67 years old. He recently decided to reverse his aging process; he set a goal to look and feel, at 70, better than how he looked and felt at 60. He has a diet regimen that he follows religiously. There are zero deviations. Once he decided to live in this way, that was it, the decision was enforced.

He also spends three hours every day in the gym pumping iron and doing his aerobics. He works four hours a day leading his vast holdings, managed by professional managers, using the Internet and Skype. The rest of his time is dedicated to family and friends, whom he chooses carefully: people who add rather than subtract energy from him—people he can learn from or laugh with.

'STOP DIGGING WHEN YOU HIT OIL'

I have never seen Dion in a bad mood. "Why waste time brooding?" is his motto. "Act on the problem, or forget it."

He has sold many of the businesses he started. "Today no one should fall in hopeless love with any business. Move on when it does not work. Stop beating a dead horse if the business is no good. And if it *is* good, stop digging when you hit oil."

In a sense, everything is black and white for him. He's very (P)-oriented, but with lots of (E)—*without* all the confusion that (E)s bring to the table. He is certainly an (E), having started so many businesses, but he is *not* an Arsonist, jumping erratically from one idea to the next. You might say he (P)s his (E).[2]

If you ask him his main priorities, he lists his health and the health of his family, followed by the health of his businesses. His goals are simple and well focused.

---

[2] For further details about the (PAEI) code, see my book *The Ideal Executive: Why You Cannot Be One and What to Do About It* (Santa Barbara, CA: Adizes Institute Publications, 2004).

I think the explanation for his lack of internal marketing is his remarkable level of commitment. Or maybe I am wrong. But I am continually wondering why most people I know do not walk their talk; they make decisions, but their implementation is weak or never occurs. Dion is unique in that he implements his decisions totally and swiftly, almost effortlessly.

George Soros, the renowned businessman and investor, must have the same characteristic: In his book *Soros on Soros: Staying Ahead of the Curve*,[3] he writes that the secret of his success is that he identifies and corrects his mistakes sooner than most people. This is the same principle as implementing decisions without hesitation.

I also find that surgeons, especially heart surgeons, have that characteristic: They do not waver between deciding and implementing. It is artists and intellectuals who "decide" but then have second and third thoughts, and whose execution, if any, resembles only vaguely their initial decision.

I know I am terrible at implementation. For me, all the excitement is in the decision-making. That is where my mind is fully engaged. Implementation is pure hard work and no fun.

Do you have a theory about why Dion is so special? Do you know people like him? What makes them so different, and how can we emulate them?

---

[3] New York: John Wiley & Sons, Inc., 1995.

How to Faithfully Apply Decisions in Personal Life; or, What Can We Learn from Dion, Part 2[1]

I N the previous chapter, "What Can We Learn from Dion?", I raised the question: Why is Dion so different? I wrote about how Dion decides and implements without wavering, without wasting energy making the transition from decision to implementation.

Most mortals, myself included, decide, but then stew and sweat, struggling back and forth about implementing the decision we already made (for instance, think about how difficult it is to actually stop smoking, even after you've decided to do it) to the point that many decisions never get implemented at all. And those decisions that do get implemented only *resemble* the original decision, and I'm using the word "resemble" loosely.

In my consulting practice for organizations, I have solved this problem.

First, we must have a united, common interest in seeing them implemented correctly. Thus, in the Adizes methodology, we assemble the CAPI (coalesced authority, power, and influence) group necessary to solve the problem; then we set them the task of solving it.

In other words, we make sure that all the interests are aligned, and then we seek a common good. This method, as those who practice Adizes know from experience, works quite well: Decisions, even some very painful ones (like major structural, corporate, organizational changes) are implemented without deviation from the original decision. Change is swift and without much wasted energy. But how can we be like Dion, applying to our personal lives what we already do for companies?

---

[1] Adizes Insights, August 2010.

Dr. Douglas Lisle, an esoteric psychologist, gave me an insight—or the beginning of an insight—that might solve this riddle. He suggested that we have difficulty implementing our decisions because we have multiple agendas (like having multiple interests in a company). It is easier when we have a single agenda. "Aha!" I said to myself, "that is exactly the case with Dion." He truly has a single agenda, which is his health. Everything else is not even a second priority.

When Everything Is a Priority

I believe (E)s have the greatest problems with implementation. (E)s want to have their cake and eat it, too. They want everything. They want to make the maximum money possible, yet also have the maximum balanced life at the same time. (E)s want to travel a lot and still have a family life; they want to work very long hours and still have well-adjusted kids. They want it all, although getting anything done requires making choices among those priorities, because time and energy are fixed entities.

They hate making choices that sacrifice their "wants," sometimes seemingly relying on a miracle to make it all happen.

Now note: When do we finally have a single agenda? Our priorities align quickly when forced on us by external factors. For example, a small heart attack will cause a shift in our priorities. After a close encounter with death, you might discover religion and become committed to a single goal: survival.

Or perhaps you go Chapter Eleven. Or maybe your wife serves you divorce papers. Now you drop everything and focus! (Obviously, these are not recommended medicines for the malady.)

Let us learn from our efforts to help companies make decisions that they do implement. Organizations do not have common interests, either. They hire us to develop a common interest, to develop common solutions to their problems, and to coach them till their problems are gone and they have the knowledge and experience to make and implement future decisions.

If we apply this to personal life, it seems to me that the solution is to find a coach: a lifestyle coach, a nutrition coach, and/or a personal trainer, depending on which commitment you need help with.

If you can't make your decisions stick, don't despair; get help. We need each other. The sooner you admit this, the sooner you will be a better person.

THE THREE PILLARS[1]

IN Jewish rabbinical teaching there is a saying (they've even made a song out of it) that goes: "*Al shlosha devarim ha olam omed*," which means, "The world is built on three pillars."

They are:

Al ha avoda: work;

Al ha Tora: the book of rules; and

Ve al gemul hasadim: acts of kindness to others.

Let's try to classify these three pillars in the (PAEI) code:[2]

Work is (P);

the book of rules (Torah) is (A);

and acts of kindness to others would be (I).

What is missing? (E).

Why?

One possible explanation that comes to my mind is that we, the Jews, have more than enough (E) already, so there's no need to make a pillar of it. Anyone else have a theory? Let me know your thoughts.

HOW TO SOLVE A CHRONIC PROBLEM

During dinner with my friend Michael Perry, an Israeli professor, I was complaining about how difficult it is for me to manage. I love to write and lecture and consult—but not to operationally manage an organization. I told him that I feel like I'm trapped in a prison of my own creation. How strange this is, I mused, because I have dedicated my professional life to freeing others from the same prison I am in, yet I cannot help myself.

He smiled and quoted a book of Jewish wisdom, *Pirkey Avot:* "*Ein ha asir*

---

[1] Adizes Insights, January 2008.

[2] For further details about the (PAEI) code, see my book *The Ideal Executive: Why You Cannot Be One and What to Do About It* (Santa Barbara, CA: Adizes Institute Publications, 2004).

metir atzmo me asurav," which is translated as: "No prisoner frees himself of his chains."

This could be the slogan for psychotherapists and all other healers, no?

We try to free ourselves from our chains and cannot do it. But we can free each other.

This reminds me of an allegory I heard somewhere:

A man dies and goes to the other world. There he is judged to have committed sins and good deeds in equal measure, and he is told he may visit both hell and heaven and then choose between them. He goes to hell and finds people sitting around a big cauldron trying to eat soup. Each person has a three-feet-long spoon and cannot feed himself. All look hungry and are suffering. He then goes to heaven, where people sit around an identical cauldron with the same soup, and each one is holding the same three-foot-long spoon, but here they are feeding each other. And guess what? They all look happy.

Chronic problems are like chains. Somehow in life, we all get entangled in some chains—like bad habits or a self-destructive style. Or we get angry easily because we live in constant fear of rejection, etc.

It is easy to pick up one chain or another, and they become chronic problems; in spite of continually trying to solve them, they are still a reality we face. And most of us feel guilty and disempowered for being chained and not being able to free ourselves. Thus, we deny those chains even exist or get very angry if someone points them out to us.

What to do? "No prisoner frees himself of his chains." Stop living in hell. Get someone to free you, and then you can free someone else. The chains that you help someone else to escape may be the same ones that had you hopelessly ensnared only a short time ago.

Life Is …

In my lectures I say that change creates problems. To solve them, we must first decide what to do; and then implement that decision.

Strategic decisions that deal with change need a complementary team to make that decision, and that, by definition, will cause conflict: because different people think differently, we do not all process information the same way. To implement a decision, we need all those who are necessary for efficient implementation to share a common interest. But that means conflict, because common interest is a rare phenomenon. It is not natural and automatic, and even when it does exist, time and change will eventually threaten it.

Now, since change is life (only with death comes the stasis of no change) and change is conflict, it follows that life itself is conflict. And what is conflict? Pain. In other words, get real. Life is pain, an ongoing process that causes pain and pain again.

Watching the movie *The Princess Bride* (which I have watched at least a dozen times because I love it with all my heart), I am always gratified when the farm boy says: "Life is pain. ... Anyone who says differently is selling something."

Absolutely.

> When you are totally at peace, you are not doing any "internal marketing...." Thus, all your energy is available to be used outside yourself.

PEACE AND LEGENDS

During the Jewish High Holidays, I had some insights while reading the prayer book.

There is a relationship between the words and thus the concepts of "holy," "whole," and "peace." Let us start with the Hebrew words.

"Peace" is *shalom* and "whole" is *shalem*. Their common root is SHL. And the insight? You are at peace when you are whole. When you are one. When you are not fighting yourself.

Now, in English, "whole" and "holy" share the same Old English root. Who is holy? One who is so whole that she is not just at peace with herself, but at peace and whole, or integrated, with the world, with space, with God. When a person is fully, totally at peace, he or she is holy. Such people are sometimes said to have an aura around their heads. Why? Because when you are totally at peace, you are not doing any "internal marketing," or what I now call "internal disintegration." Thus, all your energy is available to be used outside yourself; nothing is wasted inside. So it's no surprise that such a person projects energy outward, and that is the aura people see.

Why is that holy? Because that person can be a healer, by giving his energy to others. Jesus, then, was so much at peace with himself, so whole, and thus holy, that he could heal a child who had died, performing the miracle of bringing her back to life. He gave the child energy.

Here is another insight from the prayer book:

The words in Hebrew for "union" and for "legend" come from the same root: AGD. "Union" is *agudah* and "legend" is *agada*. My insight: to facilitate a union, to get people to become united, is not easy and natural. It is a problem, and requires work which, when done, is material for a legend.

COURAGE ...

I do not know when I first heard this remark by Winston Churchill , but I instantly loved it. It definitely endorses the rule in the Adizes methodology of waiting your turn to speak. Here it is:

"Many people think that courage is what it takes to stand up and speak. But courage is also what it takes to sit down and listen."

Amen.

PART 5

SPIRITUALITY AND RELIGION

WHAT IS MISSING?[1]

I ONCE had a client whose behavior was typical of thousands of other executives: He was managing a very successful empire, taking risks, working harder and harder.

"What for?" I asked him. "You have all the money you may ever need."

"So I can get myself a bigger plane," he said with a smile. Eventually he owned the biggest, most luxurious private jet. Then he bought an expensive beach compound for the summers, and a lavish 182-foot yacht, and a compound in the mountains, and began looking for an even bigger mansion with a helicopter pad.

It reminded me of women who have hundreds of shoes and keep buying more. They shop for more and more clothes, more and more jewelry ... what they have is never enough.

What are they missing? I suggest that they are missing true meaning in their lives. It is as if they have a hole in the middle of their chest that they are trying to fill with material possessions.

When we lack a spiritual center, we try to fill it up with possessions. But it never suffices, because a spiritual "hole" has no bottom.

When people have spiritual meaning in their lives, their interest in material possessions takes a back seat. For instance, material needs have no meaning whatsoever to those who are candidates for sainthood.

What I am suggesting here is that the executive I described above has no spiritual meaning in his life. He has a hole and until he fills this hole with meaning, he will continue building a material empire. But no matter how big his empire might become, he will still feel unfulfilled.

Now imagine a finishing school for young ladies where they are taught to measure their success in life by how many shoes they have and how expensive their clothes and jewelry are. You would feel aghast, no?

---

[1] Adizes Insights, October 2008.

That is exactly what business schools do. They teach students to measure success exclusively by measuring EBITA, earnings per share, and how much stockholders' equity has increased.

We are creating a class of rich, unhappy people. To find peace in their lives, they need to develop their spiritual lives independently, because they sure don't get it from business.

Many people confuse spirituality with religion. Big mistake. Some religions, or the fringes of that religion, have lost their spiritual orientation; they preach killing and destruction. "Spiritual," to me, means feeling part of something larger than oneself by adhering to moral principles that are absolute and timeless.

NURTURE THE HEAD *AND* THE HEART

Let me give you an example from my consulting experience:

Years ago, I had a client company that produced respiratory equipment for hospitals. They had a quality-control problem. Their question was how many new quality control people they should hire.

I suggested an alternative solution: Take the workers from Production, those whom everyone looked up to, to the neighborhood hospital to visit children who had respiratory diseases. Ask them to take pictures of these kids while they are breathing with the aid of the company's equipment. Bring those pictures back to the company and hang them everywhere.

What might that do to the quality of the products they manufactured?

We teach our future business leaders numbers, concepts, and theories. We fill their heads, but their hearts might be empty. Schools of management that prepare our future powerful leaders nurture the head but neglect the heart. These people might, later in life, finally pay attention to their hearts and donate their accumulated shoes and jewels, or money, to charity, but that is like atoning for a wasted life.

I have a suggestion to make: No one should be admitted to a school of business or get accredited as a professional leader unless he has exhibited concern for the world beyond himself.

Today, leading business schools require that the applicant have prior business experience. In the future, I suggest that to be admitted, he must also have community experience working as a community organizer, or serving in the Peace Corps, or volunteering for a not-for-profit organization.

And during his management education, he must take a summer internship helping people who need help: building houses with Habitat for Humanity; working in poverty-stricken neighborhoods; raising funds for local medical centers that provide free care for the indigent; etc.

Management and business schools are doing a disservice by offering these one-sided programs. It is time for schools to train leaders with brain *and* heart, for the sake of society and our own happiness.

> Many people confuse spirituality with religion. Big mistake.

Without spiritual meaning, life is empty; No mater how much we have, we still will not feel complete.

LEADING CHANGE FOR
SUSTAINABLE INNOVATION[1]

DEAN Danica Purg, faculty, guests, students, friends:
Thank you for inviting me to this celebration. I am an old friend of Danica's and I have been invited to give presentations to this wonderful creation, the IEDC [International Executive Development Center], many times since its inception.

And I have been watching with awe the wonderful work Danica has done. If there is an ideal example of leadership for sustainable innovation, Danica is that example.

Thank you, Danica, for giving me the floor once again to express myself in front of this wonderful audience.

I was asked to make a presentation on "Leading Change for Sustainable Innovation."

Each word in this title is very popular today. It has become a fad at management retreats and elsewhere to discuss the concepts of leadership, sustainability, change, innovation.

But is this what is *really* important?

Let us discuss.

INNOVATIVE, PROFITABLE, AND SUSTAINABLE

In a company that produces oral hygiene products, a young business school graduate is hired. Eager to prove his worth, he comes up with a recommendation for management on how to increase profitability.

His recommendation is to enlarge the hole in the toothpaste tube, so that with the same squeeze, consumers would get more toothpaste out

---

[1] Speech given at the 25th anniversary of the founding of the IEDC, celebrated in Slovenija, October 14, 2010.

of the tube. This would increase the consumption of toothpaste by 100 percent.

And since the cost of making a bigger hole in the tube is close to nothing, the increase in revenues would correspond to an almost 100 percent increase in profits.

What a great idea. What a genius. The kid gets a promotion, and a bonus.

Now, is this truly an innovation?

I think so.

Is it sustainable?

Why not? It would produce profits, and most consumers probably would not notice that their toothpaste is being used up faster than usual. Even if they did notice, they would probably blame themselves for squeezing the tube too hard.

Does the young man's innovation qualify as leadership? It would probably be considered as such. The kid stood out in the crowd and produced profitable change in the company.

It was sustainable. It was leadership. It was innovation. It was profitable.

Is this what we should do as managers, as business leaders?

I ask you.

> Look at how quickly a chain of outlets selling cupcakes expands, or a chain that sells fried food. That is how you make money: You sell what people want to buy.

Uninnovative, Unsustainable, and Unprofitable

Now, let us take another example. There is a health center in California that promotes a vegan diet. (This, like the previous anecdote, is a true story, ladies and gentlemen.)

At this health center, the doctors try to change our habit of eating animal products, oil, salt, sugar, and processed food—and eat, instead, what our ancestors in the Stone Age ate: vegetables, fruits, and nuts.

Would *this* be considered an innovation?

I do not think so. Not for taking us back 2,000 years.

Is it sustainable?

Probably not. One of the goals of this vegetarian diet is to lose weight.

But 97 percent of people who try to lose weight fail to do so.

Nor does the center make a profit. How many people do you think will pay a large amount of money to go there and eat vegetables and fruit all day long? There is no money in this business. If there were, hundreds of such centers would open up all over the place, like mushrooms after the rain.

But look at how quickly a chain of outlets selling cupcakes expands, or a chain that sells fried food. *That* is how you make money: You sell what people want to buy. You innovate something that has value—something the market approves of.

Is that so?

WHAT CONSTITUTES LEADERSHIP?

The toothpaste company is making more money, all right, but it is also wasting resources. Is that good for society? You tell me.

The vegetarian center is losing money while struggling to heal people of obesity and its related diseases—diabetes, heart attacks, strokes, lupus, and other inflammations. Is *that* good for society, even though it is not making money? You tell me.

Making money should *not* be the goal. Innovation should *not* be the goal. Sustainability should *not* be the goal. Even leadership should not be the goal.

They are all means to achieve the *real* goal. But we often forget what the real goal is, and should be.

Sociologists tell us that the purpose of both humans and organizations is survival.

Is that so?

Look at how we eat. Look at how we treat our air, water, and earth. Look at the crime rate. Look at how often you hear about children murdering their own parents.

And what about the nuclear devices we have developed, which can destroy society and the entire world as we know it?

Are we doing what it takes to survive, or are we slowly but surely moving toward the destruction of our civilization?

The medical profession says the goal of the human organism is to reproduce itself. We are reproductive machines.

OK. That sounds to me like another way of saying "survival of the species"—a goal that is slightly broader than the one sociology offers us.

But is it true? Are we doing what it takes to prolong the life of our species? Are we leaving a better world than the world our parents gave us?

Technology-wise, yes. We definitely have it better than our ancestors. Medicine has advanced beyond what our grandparents could even dream about.

But is it a better world?

I suggest that it is not.

> *The benefit of what we do must be higher than the cost—and I'm talking about the cost not just to the company but to the world, to society, to our children.*

Overall, we are destroying the world we live in: polluting the air, the water, and the earth. Our children will have to go to a zoo to see animals that today we can still see all around us. Our grandchildren will never see some of the flowers whose scents we appreciate today, because they are becoming extinct right now—*this moment, as we speak.* They will never see certain species of fish and birds. Because of air pollution, they will never stand atop a city skyscraper and see an urban panorama stretching for miles in every direction.

What are we doing?

THE REAL GOAL

What *should* be our goal?

Tikkun olam. That should be the goal. *Tikkun olam* is the ancient Hebrew explanation for why we are here on this planet.

And what does it mean? The literal translation is: "To repair the world"—in other words, to leave it a better world when we die than the way we found it when we were born.

Why "to repair"? Because of entropy. Because of change. The world is constantly changing, but not for the better—unless we take the initiative and proactively *make* change for the better.

Our garden will become a messy jungle of weeds unless we tend it. Our car will fall apart unless it is maintained. Our marriage will lose its creative intimacy if we ignore its demands.

We have to work the garden. Repair the car. Invest time in our marriage. Work on our community. Work for our country. Help heal the earth.

Tikkun olam—to heal the world, to leave it a better place than the place we inherited—should be the goal.

Innovation, sustainability, leadership, yes—but they must be viewed through the following prism: Does our innovation heal the world, or does it damage the world?

All our actions should have a spiritual criterion.

Profits should not be the goal. They should be the *constraint*: Of course we do not want to go bankrupt, but the benefit of what we do must be higher than the cost—and I'm talking about the cost not just to the company but to the world, to society, to our children.

It is not true that we pass the world on to our children. In fact, we are borrowing the world from our children. We are leaving them a dirty, messy world that they will have to clean up in order to survive; and a social security deficit they will not be able to pay.

And it is all coming from the single erroneous, misguided concept of profit as a goal.

Innovation, yes—but for what?

Sustainability, yes—but for what?

Leadership, sure—but for what?

Let us not forget what we are really in this world for. Let us not forget that as children of God, we are here to serve love and not hate—to serve the good of the world—because our days are numbered and we cannot take anything with us.

So what counts is not what we take, but what we leave behind.

Thank you.

CAN ENERGY BE INFINITE?[1]

I WOULD like to share with you one of the many insights I had while on a meditation retreat in Denmark.

In my books and blogs, I have frequently spoken of one of my principles of success: Energy is fixed, and any part of that energy that is wasted on internal destructive conflicts is not available to compete in the marketplace.

Since energy is fixed, the more energy is wasted on internal disintegration, the less is available for external integration, where success is measured.

Now, notice that the formula is based on the assumption that energy is fixed. Unless that is so, the formula will not work. But I always felt comfortable with the assumption that energy is fixed. That is what the theory of physics tells us.

Energy is fixed.

Energy is fixed?

Here is a different view.

Imagine that energy is infinite. Not fixed. Infinite. It can all be available to us, as long as we do not have filters and barriers that work to reduce its availability.

What are those barriers and filters? They are the internal "noises" between our ears, which distract us from our connection to the universe and this endless energy. It is our internal disintegration.

The noisier the chatter in our heads, the less we feel and accept the Lord, and the more we start usurping God's powers by trying to manage our lives independently of Him/Her. The noisier the chatter, the less energy we'll have to tackle the world and its problems.

We will have *endless* energy when we accept God. When we realize we are *not* the center of the world. That the Lord is the center, and we just have to follow Him/Her. When we surrender to the Lord, that is when we

---

[1] Excerpted from Adizes Insights, January 2008.

and God are united. And that is when we are the most powerful, and thus the most successful.

> The noisier the chatter [in our heads], the less energy we'll have to tackle the world and its problems.

This conclusion feels counter-intuitive at first. Is it not true that in order to succeed, one has to take his destiny in his hands, controlling his own destiny as much as possible? As a path to success, surrender—to anyone or anything—does not feel right.

But look at truly spiritual people: They are calmer than the rest of us. They trust God, thus they have less conflict with the world they live in. They can hold their breath underwater—which is how life feels when one is stressed—longer. They have patience. Their minds are less preoccupied with irrelevant disturbances. By totally renouncing control, they are in full control.

How is that for understanding duality?

WE NEED A NEW,
'UMBRELLA' RELIGION[1]

T ODAY, I read that a rabbi requested that the Seattle airport authorities add a Hanukah menorah to their Christmas holiday decorations.

That is interesting.

What would happen if a Christian religious leader asked the Tel Aviv airport to add a Christmas tree to its Hanukah display?

There would be a religious uproar in Israel. There is no chance the airport authorities would comply.

Why? Because Israel is a Jewish state. The United States, however, *is not* a Christian state.

Hmmm! We are different, eh?

Let us discuss.

I have difficulty with two sentences in my Jewish prayer book; I always skip them or remain silent when it is time to recite them: *"Ata behartanu"* ("You have chosen us"); and *"Baruch ata adonay she lo asanu ke goyey ha adama"* ("Blessed is the Lord who did not make us like the non-Jews").

I have difficulty with this apparent sense of superiority. It can cause resentment and rejection: A force in one direction calls for a responding force in the opposite direction.

But wait a moment. Is it only the Jews who are separatists and believe they are superior? No. All religions have rules and rituals meant to foster separation and seclusion.

Religious Jews cannot eat food prepared by non-Jews, because they eat only kosher food. They live within walking distance of the synagogue, because it is forbidden to ride or drive on the Sabbath, with the result that they tend to cluster together in a small, segregated section of town.

---

[1] Adizes Insights, December 2006.

Furthermore, they speak languages, Yiddish and Hebrew, that no one else shares.

And the Orthodox, the very religious Jews, will actually disown their own son or daughter, and mourn as if the child had died, if that child marries out of the faith.

But what about the other religions? Muslims are required to fast from sunrise to sunset during the month of Ramadan, while Catholics do a combination of fasting, prayer, and penitence during the forty days before Easter. All religions have rules and rituals that set them apart from others.

PRIDE, NOT FEAR

Religions, in other words, do everything they can to prevent assimilation. It is my belief that all those detailed rules and rituals were designed to counter religious leaders' fear that if their believers are not deliberately forced to be different, they will eventually lose their unique beliefs and become the same.

Hmmm....

Can't we be different without fear of assimilation—without having to reject others because they are not like us?

Take me, for instance. I feel Jewish and I am proud of it, and would like my children and grandchildren to be Jewish, to continue a commitment made thousands of years ago to a certain set of values, a certain attitude toward life, and the principle of *tikkun olam* ("to repair the world"; in other words, to work responsibly to create a better world).

But I do it out of pride, not out of fear.

My pride in being Jewish means I need no rituals to isolate and separate me from non-Jews. Nor do I object to or fear an airport that displays only a Christmas tree—as long as no one forces that tree into my home. At home is where I have my menorah.

I admire all the other religions that have values that deserve admiration. In fact, I think the world needs a *new* religion—an "umbrella" religion that accepts all religions as equally legitimate.

Like a hand: Each finger is different, but they still work together.

A CHRISTMAS INSIGHT[1]

FIRST of all, for those of you who celebrate Christmas, I wish you a merry one. For those who celebrated Hanukah, I pray you had a great one. And for those who practice no religion, a wonderful season's greeting to you.

May we all celebrate surrounded by family, by love and friendship, and may we remember to celebrate our gratitude for being alive.

Now, the Insight:

Do all of you realize that Jesus was a Jew? In his era, and for two hundred years thereafter, there were no Christians. Those who believed in him as the messiah ("savior") were Jews. Peter was Jewish. So was Paul. So were all the Apostles.

> Being the messiah required absolute compliance with God's laws, so Jesus must have been a very religious Jew.

In the history of Judaism, the belief that a messiah had arrived was not unprecedented. Two hundred years after Jesus' death, some Jews believed Bar Kokhba was the messiah. Fifteen hundred years later, thousands of Jews believed Sabbatai Zevi was the messiah. And today, as I am writing this Insight, there are thousands of Hassidim—very religious Jews called the Lubavitch, or Chabad, movement—who believe that their rabbi, Rabbi Menachem Schneerson, is the messiah.

The fact that they believe in a messiah does not make them non-Jews. They consider themselves very Jewish.

Jesus was in fact a practicing Jew—very much so. Not only was he one of the chosen people, but, since he believed himself to be God's son, he would have felt he was the chosen among the chosen.

Being the messiah required absolute compliance with God's laws, so Jesus must have been a very religious Jew. He must have been circumcised;

---

[1] Adizes Insights, December 2009.

he must have celebrated his bar mitzvah. And he must have covered his head. All those painters and sculptors who have depicted Jesus for the past two thousand years should go back to the drawing board, make him look more Jewish (if there is such a thing as a Jewish look), and cover his head.

Jesus had a Jewish mother. And a Jewish father.

The Rift Between Jews and Christians

For 70 years, those who worshiped Jesus considered themselves to be a reform movement within Judaism, and when non-Jews joined that group, they were actually joining the Jewish religion. The *Jewish* Christian movement did not begin to dissipate until 70 A.D., when the Romans destroyed the Temple in Jerusalem and exiled the Jews.

Then, around 132 A.D., many Jews decided that Bar Kokhba, the leader of a briefly successful revolt against Rome, was the messiah. As a result, those who worshiped Jesus formally split from the Jewish people, and founded Christianity.

When I was a student at Hebrew University in Jerusalem, I worked as a tour guide. It was always an amazing experience to guide religious Christians. Just imagine how they reacted when I took them to the room where, according to the tradition, Jesus had his last supper. Or when we walked the same path along which Jesus endured the twelve stations.

I lived about hundred yards from the valley from which, according to tradition, the tree was cut to produce the cross on which he was crucified. And I used to take my tourists to a hill called the Mount of Beatitudes, where Jesus gave the Sermon on the Mount and then walked on water in the Sea of Galilee. We also visited the cave in Nazareth where Jesus is believed to have lived as a child.

My point is that Jesus, all his life, was a member of the Jewish tribe and lived as a Jew among Jews.

But I never gave much thought to this fact until recently, when I saw a CNN program about the early Christians. Since I had known it but needed reminding, I thought some of you might also appreciate the reminder.

Merry Christmas to you all, again and again!

WHERE IS GOD?[1]

DURING the Jewish "High Holidays" when I go to the synagogue, I am always taken aback by the descriptions of God in the prayer book. He (the Deity is somehow always male) sits on a high throne, *bameromim* ("up there somewhere in space.") He sees everything; is all-powerful; arranges the stars and the moon and the sun; can sometimes be forgiving, but can also be very vengeful; and so on.

God is not alone up there. There are angels to serve him and, according to the Bible, the Devil is also in the vicinity, busy trying to undermine God's work by ignoring or refusing to obey His instructions.

Recently I watched a program about Greek mythology on public TV, and I noticed that the descriptions of Zeus sounded awfully familiar: Zeus, too, is all-powerful. Zeus has lesser gods to do his bidding, while our God has angels. And just as the Devil challenges God, the lesser gods sometimes defy or ignore Zeus's commands.

But I felt uncomfortable with these descriptions, and I wondered: Where is God? *What* is God?

SERVING GOD OR DEFYING GOD

In another recent blog, I presented the idea that the human body has no manager. The system manages itself.

If we used this as an analogy, we would conclude that there's no God, no Zeus-type figure arranging the world up there, watching our every move through His Godly binoculars. Perhaps God is a system, and every part of the system is part of God. This analogy makes sense to me.

And what is a system? A system comprises not only its components, but also the relationship among those components.

What makes the components of any system work well together? From

---

[1] Adizes Insights, December 2010.

Adizes theory, we already know the answer: synergetic and symbiotic relationships, with mutual trust and respect (MT&R).

If God is a system, composed of sub-systems and their interactions, then nurturing MT&R means serving God, and violating MT&R may be defying God!

Let's take this idea even further: If MT&R requires absolute integration, and if absolute integration, as I believe, is *love*, then God is love! In other words, those who hate in the name of God are not serving God at all.

Many theologians have reached the same conclusions. I now understand them.

WHERE WAS GOD
DURING THE HOLOCAUST?[1]

A READER'S comment on the blog where I posted the previous chapter, "Where Is God?," shook me up.

For those of you who did not read the comments section, he or she wrote: "My God was cremated during the Holocaust."

He is not alone in feeling that way. Many Holocaust survivors, including my own father, felt that way. They questioned God's existence: How could God allow Auschwitz, allow the Nazis to incinerate innocent children, not to mention the murder of many rabbis who honestly and faithfully worshipped God?

Where was God when this was going on?

The God the Holocaust survivors denounce is a Zeus-like God who fell asleep at the wheel, allowing these atrocities to occur.

Yes, Kalmar, I agree with you: that kind of God, Zeus-like, all-powerful and responsible for everything that happens on earth, does not exist.

THE SYSTEM OF GOD

The God I believe in is a system, governed by a formula that makes the world function, now and forever.

As an analogy, take the human body. When we get sick, why doesn't our brain fix the malady, especially if it is life-threatening? Why did it even allow the malady to penetrate our body? Where was the brain?

That all-powerful brain does not exist. What does exist is a system of organs that interact and a formula that directs that interaction. For instance, if you eat, sleep, and exercise regularly, you will be sick less often and live longer. If you are eating sugar, oil, salt, and processed foods excessively, it will make you obese and eventually very sick. There is no external "manager" of

---

[1] Adizes Insights, December 2010.

the body, mind, emotions, and spirit. They are all self-managed by a formula.

Who should protect our bodies? *We* should. Stop expecting Papa to take care of you. Likewise, we are also responsible for what happens here on earth. All that God is, is a system of rules; if we do not follow them, we will eventually find ourselves in trouble; if we do follow them, we will not get into trouble.

Who created the formula? No one. Do not go back to Zeus again looking for a creator or manager. The formula evolved and is still evolving, and we are perpetually trying to understand it.

THE FORMULA

My understanding of the formula that governs the world is that it is absolute, holistic love—in other words, total integration. And integration is a function of MT&R.

So where was God during the Holocaust? The formula explains what happened: The Holocaust was a manifestation of disintegration: political, social, and religious disintegration. Racism is one of the causes of disintegration, as well as a manifestation of a lack of trust and respect for others. The Holocaust happened because love was replaced by hate.

If you accept that God is a system of formulas composed of parts and relationships, then the Holocaust and God can co-exist, like the brain co-exists with diseases of the body.

To worship God is to worship love of those who are different, to love nature and treat it with respect, to love stones, water, air—to love everything. Limitless love is God. The more you love, the closer you get to God.

But love has to be protected. Why? Because it is easy to hate, and much more difficult to love. When hate raises its ugly head, those who love must not close their eyes or look away, letting hate escalate until it is too late. That is what almost happened with Hitler: If Germany, instead of the Allies, had won the nuclear race (which it almost did), those of us who survived would all be speaking German today.

Right now, Iran is developing a nuclear device. Its leaders are openly threatening to wipe Israel off the map. If *that* Holocaust happens, would we again accuse God of failing to protect us? Maybe *we* should take the responsibility for what is happening.

Are we protecting love or allowing hate to rule the world? God is watching.

Daring to Think
'Out of the Box'[1]

T HE formula I discovered that predicts success, no matter how it is
defined, posits that success is a function of external integration divided
by internal disintegration.

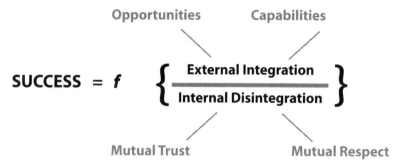

External integration is a function of how well the opportunities in the
marketplace are matched with the capabilities of the company. The better
the two are matched, the better the company is integrated with its market,
as measured by market share and repeated sales.

Integrating company capabilities to market needs requires managerial
energy, and we know that energy is fixed at any point in time. Energy that
should be available for external integration can easily be wasted by internal
disintegration.

Internal disintegration is a function of mutual trust and respect. The less
mutual trust and respect in the culture of the company, the more internal
disintegration there will be, and thus the less energy will be available to deal
with integrating the company externally.

---

[1] Adizes Insights, May 2010.

A company is in its Prime[2] condition, and thus positioned for sustainable success, when it is integrated both externally and internally.

The above is all old stuff. Now, the latest insight:

THE IDEAL INTEGRATION

When is a person most integrated? Wouldn't you agree that it is during those few seconds of an orgasm when making love?

During those seconds, we are "lost in space"—we do not know where we are, or what time it is, or anything else.

During those seconds, we are fully integrated with everything—and aware of nothing.

Please notice the apparent contradiction: It is as if nothing and everything meet.

> A true spiritual person is not someone who follows the rules of religion blindly, but one who is constantly asking questions and struggling to understand the meaning of God.

What happens when a star gets sucked into a black hole? Its mass gets more and more dense—i.e., integrated—until everything becomes nothing, or maybe it is more accurate to say that nothing and everything become the same. At least that is how I understand it, and I might be wrong, having no training on the subject.

That nothing and everything "meet" should not come as a surprise. The earth is not flat, so going in one direction will bring you all the way around to your starting point.

On a flat earth, you would have opposites at two ends, like love and hate, cold and hot, black and white, or integration and disintegration.

But on a round earth, there is no beginning and thus no end: When you have a fever (are hot), what happens to your body? You shiver (feel cold). At the North Pole, looking for too long at the white snow can make you blind (see blackness). When you close your eyes in total darkness, you see white dots. Extreme love might be the beginning of resentment, and extreme hatred the beginning of love.

So why shouldn't extreme everything be the beginning of nothing, and extreme nothing the beginning of everything?

---

[2] For more information on the theory of lifecycles, see Ichak Adizes, *Managing Corporate Lifecycles* (Santa Barbara, CA: Adizes Institute Publications, 2004).

When we meditate, we learn to "go in" and totally calm our minds. If we can free our minds from thinking about anything (think nothing), we may find God—which to me is everything.

A NEVER-ENDING TASK

OK, so what?

In management, if my theory of success holds, we should try to reach this point of total internal and external integration. But if this insight is correct, then total integration will be the beginning of disintegration.

It makes sense to me, because of change. Both the external and internal environments constantly change, making continuous, steady integration impossible.

It is not a question of good or bad. It is what it is, and managers should see this as a challenge: to work on integration, continuously and forever, knowing that it is a task for Sisyphus—a never-ending job.

Total integration, total happiness, total health, anything "total" does not exist for long in a dynamic system, which is what life is—life is continuous change.

> Total integration, total happiness, total health, anything "total" does not exist for long in a dynamic system.

The role of management is to continuously work on integration and, once achieved, cause *dis*integration—or what Joseph Shumpeter called "creative destruction"[3]—by leading change. And repeat the cycle again and again. (This is another argument for the need of a complementary team: one causes change and thus disintegrates; the other tries to bring the pieces together.)

Now: Back to absolute integration, i.e., God: Just as in management, where we can achieve integration only by continuously integrating what naturally has disintegrated through the life forces of change, we can only find God through the process of seeking God. We cannot find him and "rest." We can only continuously seek him. In seeking enlightenment, we are enlightened.

Who is truly a servant of God? A true spiritual person is not someone

---

[3] Shumpeter first coined this phrase in his book *Capitalism, Socialism, and Democracy* (New York, Harper & Row, Inc., 1943), to denote a "process of industrial mutation that incessantly revolutionizes the economic structure from within, incessantly destroying the old one, incessantly creating a new one."

who follows the rules of religion blindly, but one who is constantly asking questions and struggling to understand the meaning of God. It is the seeker, who also recognizes the fact that he will never get to a final answer.

If the above argument makes sense, then I wonder if those who claim to have exclusive knowledge of God and God's laws, and persecute those whose interpretations and beliefs are different, are really serving God? I question their spirituality.

Since life is change, and change causes disintegration, the way to live is to seek the elusive, never-to-be-found total integration. And that means that the answer to life is to continually ask.

MT&R, GOD, AND THE DEVIL: CONSTRUCTIVE AND DESTRUCTIVE CONFLICT[1]

L OOK at the Adizes change management map on page 142. It illustrates that to manage problems, you have to make decisions, for which you need a complementary team. And you have to implement those decisions, for which you need to consider the common interests of all the parties required for implementation.

Both decision-making and implementation create conflict. A complementary team means, by definition, that there will be style differences in how we process information and how we judge situations. That also means conflict. And there will be additional conflicts because we don't always have common interests: We, as people, change; our interests change; and the conditions we live in change. Thus, common interests do not remain common over time. Even if there was a common interest at the start of a relationship, we cannot take it for granted that it will remain that way.

So conflict is inevitable. The more change there is, the more conflict there will be. Conflict can destroy people, marriages, businesses, whole societies. So what are we to do? Should we stop change to avoid destructive conflict? Several political theories and religions try to do that, but without success. To stop all conflicts, one must first stop all change. That is utopian. No one can "freeze" the whole world forever.

Is it impossible, then, to stop the progress along the road to destructive conflict? Not at all. We simply must find the exit that points toward *con*structive conflict.

---

[1] Adizes Insights, July 2007. From a speech given at the Founder Session Presentation, the 29th Annual Adizes Convention, in Palic, Serbia, July 6, 2007.

Granted, the road to *de*structive conflict is easier. Think about how easy it is to destroy a building versus how time-consuming and costly it is to build it. Notice how difficult it is to build a relationship and how easy it is to destroy it—sometimes in seconds.

You have to make a choice between the easy road toward destructive conflict, or the much more arduous one toward constructive conflict. Depending on the choices we make, we can create constructive or destructive change. We can have longer or shorter lives—as people, as a country, or as a civilization. Living in this new jungle, we can choose to accelerate life or to accelerate death.

But how can we break the code that guides us to constructive conflict? Which way does the compass point? What should we be conscious of? What understanding must we have in order to lengthen the life of our marriage, our company, or our civilization?

We know from the Adizes change map that we must watch for the exit sign that says "Mutual Trust and Respect," or MT&R. And more and more, it appears to me that MT&R *is* the code. MT&R explains the nature of conflict in all systems, not just organizations but also people, marriage, society, and even how long life on this planet will exist.

What is MT&R? It is the variable that enables integration.

And why is integration so important?

Everything in this world is a system, and by definition every system is composed of sub-systems. When there is change, those sub-systems do not change in synchronicity. Thus, change, by definition, causes disintegration, and problems are the manifestation of this disintegration.

Now, if disintegration is the cause of all problems, then the antidote to all problems is integration. "Wholeness or illness," say the psychiatrists. If we are to heal the world, we have to make it whole, which requires integration. But not through sameness; we do it through the integration of *differences*—and for that, MT&R is indispensable.

A Leap of Faith

Now let us make a leap of faith: What is absolute integration? Love!

And what is the prerequisite for love? Mutual trust and respect. There might be passion, there might be sexual attraction, but there is no love without MT&R.

Let us keep abstracting: What is absolute love? For me, it is God. Think about the fact that there is no cursing or hate or disrespect permitted in churches and synagogues. What *are* the messages from the pulpit? Love. Forgiveness. Mutual trust and respect. If you analyze the Ten Commandments, they all have one common denominator: They all promote MT&R.

Read the Old Testament. How should you treat the ox you use for work? With respect. How should you treat the convert, the *ger*, who inhabits your city? With respect. And you must always leave a part of your land for the poor to harvest, so they will have something to eat.

What should we think about those who missed the exit to MT&R, or who deliberately chose to go in the direction of destructive conflict? What about them?

> There is a little bit of God in all of us, and there is a little bit of the Devil in all of us.

Here is a thought: Although God is absolute integration, absolute love, God is not alone. There is God, and there is the Devil. It is the Devil that leads us toward the destructive road.

I believe that both exist. And I suggest that both of them, jointly, created the world. Not God alone. We were created in the image of both: There is a little bit of God in all of us, and there is a little bit of the Devil in all of us. The moon has its white, lit side *and* its dark side, and all of us have both light and darkness in us, influencing the choices we make.

God is love and forgiveness, and forgiveness and love is what? Integration. Being inspired means being united with a higher consciousness, which gives us energy.

And what does the Devil stand for? Hate, revenge, evil—which are all causes or manifestations of disintegration that take away or dissipate energy. Did you know that medical journals report that people in healthy relationships get fewer colds?

All human beings experience both feelings: love and hate. The question is: Whom do we worship with the choices we make? Which of these feelings do we follow?

THE DIFFERENCE BETWEEN FUSION AND INTEGRATION

I suggest that some religions use the name of God, but actually worship the Devil. Their actions speak loud and clear: They will behead you if you are different, or exile you if you do not share their beliefs. They have no trust

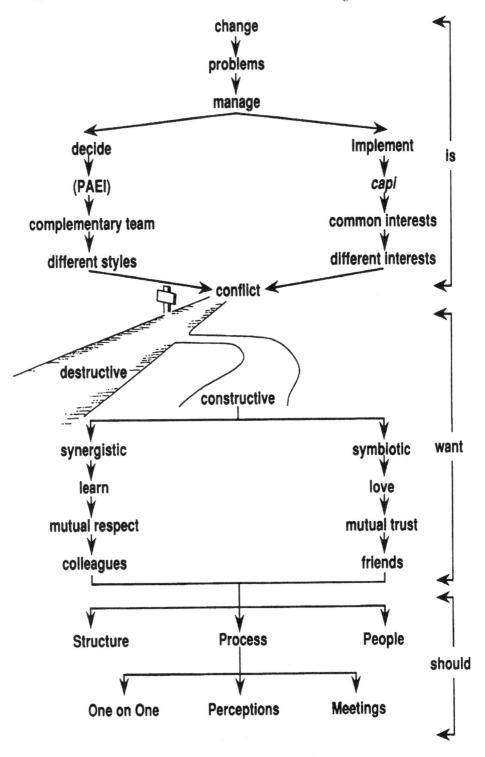

or respect for those who are different; in fact, they preach revenge, death, and destruction to anyone who thinks or acts differently. I am not referring just to today's fundamentalist Muslims. The Spanish Inquisition, perpetrated by Catholics during the Middle Ages, was no better.

Some political fanatics behave that way, too: the Fascists, the Communists. By insisting that we should all be the same, those religions and political ideologies *appear* to be fostering integration. Ironically, however, they are fostering *dis*integration. Why? Because we cannot all be the same, no matter how much these extremists use murder, exile, and terror to impose their will. They are preaching fusion, not integration, and fusion can never be achieved among people with free will.

Here is the proof: Even among themselves, extremists do not find the absolute sameness they insist upon. They are continually fighting each other, because such differences are inevitable.

What is needed is not fusion but the integration of differences: *constructive diversity*.

Not all diversity is constructive. Some political parties use the freedom of choice that constructive diversity offers in order to *destroy* diversity. These are the anti-democratic parties that use democracy to get into power, only to abolish democracy immediately afterward. The Nazis did that. Hamas is doing it now.

Mutual trust and respect is the key. I am italicizing the word "*mutual.*" Anti-democratic parties and exclusive religions command, but do not grant, trust and respect to those who are different.

> The moon has its white, lit side and its dark side, and all of us have both light and darkness in us, influencing the choices we make.

With MT&R—with integration instead of fusion of our differences—we can work together, not *in spite of* our differences but *because* of them. We enrich each other with our differences.

Thus, we must learn to practice MT&R. We need to understand how to apply MT&R to the individual, the family, the organizational, and even the global level.

Why is it necessary to apply it to everything? Because everything is interrelated. You cannot apply MT&R on the personal level and not apply it at the family level; or apply it to the family but not to the organization you work for; or practice it at the organizational level in a community where mistrust and disrespect are the norm. It simply will not work as well, because the sphere where you do *not* apply MT&R will undermine the sphere where you *do* apply it.

You cannot sustain a democratic organization in a dictatorial regime, or a dictatorial organization in a democratic regime. Inevitably one system will undermine and eventually destroy the other.

Worshiping God means love, and love means accepting and nurturing differences through MT&R. Imposing sameness looks like an attempt at integration but actually serves the Devil instead of God, since absolute sameness can never be achieved. Imposing sameness promotes hate and destruction; thus, it is a destructive rather than a constructive force.

POSTSCRIPT[2]

After this column appeared on my blog several months ago, I got a lot of feedback from some readers who were not happy with my argument—which, in effect, challenged the principles of monotheism.

Well, apparently I am not the only one with this idea. There was an ancient Persian religion called Zoroastrianism, founded by Zarathustra, that holds the belief that both an evil divinity and a good one are at work in the universe.

Scholars of religion characterize Zoroastrianism as dualism. And guess what? I am finding that dualism explains a lot of what I wonder about: night/day, breathe-in/breathe-out, cold/hot, hate/love, black/white.... Everything has its opposite, its twin.

There is so much to learn. ...

---

[2] Excerpted from Adizes Insights, October 2007.

Afterword

A Question for My Readers[1]

TWENTY-SOME years ago, I took a vacation in a place called Capitan Lafitte, which was somewhere between Playa del Carmen and Cancun, Mexico.

We slept in *palapas* on the sand. There was no electricity, no phones, no television. We woke up with the sunrise, snorkeled, walked on the beach collecting seashells, and talked a lot. After sundown, we sat around a fire, talked some more, did some singing, and went to sleep.

We ate the fish that had been caught that day and the vegetables bought from the farmers' market that day. It was a vacation I will never forget.

I went looking for it last year. It's gone. There is a building like a Motel 6 there now instead.

Also twenty years ago, I went on a two-week walking safari with my sons. We walked and canoed down the Zambezi River. For two weeks, we saw no one besides the small group we were with and our guide. We slept out in sleeping bags around a fire. I will never forget the sky at night: an endless number of stars twinkling from above. I have never seen so many stars before or since.

> *I will never forget the sky at night: an endless number of stars twinkling from above. I have never seen so many stars before or since.*

The only sounds we heard were the sounds of nature. Time slowed down: You felt as if it was already afternoon when in reality it was only 9 a.m.

What happened to these places?

I am desperately trying to find one. At one point I thought I had found it in a remote hotel in Mexico—but no luck: canned music was endlessly piped

---

[1] Adizes Insights, June 2010.

in, everywhere, at least sixteen hours a day, to "relax" me.

Does anyone know of a place like the ones I am describing above? A place where human hands have not yet interfered to "enrich" my experience? No Wi-Fi. No phones. No television, and, yes, no electricity.

If it does not exist, could someone please create one?

Please. ...

ABOUT THE ADIZES INSTITUTE

FOR the past 35 years, the Adizes Institute has been committed to equipping visionary leaders, management teams, and agents of change to become champions of their industries and markets. These leaders have successfully established a collaborative organizational culture by using Adizes' pragmatic tools and concepts to achieve peak performance.

Adizes specializes in guiding leaders of organizations (CEOs, top management teams, boards, owners) to quickly and effectively resolve such issues as:

- Difficulties in executing good decisions.
- Making the transition from entrepreneurship to professional management.
- Difficulties in aligning the structure of the organization to achieve its strategic intent.
- "Bureaucratizing": the organization is getting out of touch with its markets and beginning to lose entrepreneurial vitality.
- Conflicts among founders, owners, board members, partners, and family members.
- Internal management team conflicts and "politics" severe enough to inhibit the success of the business.
- Growing pains.
- Culture clashes between companies undergoing mergers or acquisitions.

Adizes also offers comprehensive training and certification for change leaders who wish to incorporate into their practice the Adizes methodologies for managing change.

Adizes is the primary sponsor of the Adizes Graduate School, a non-profit teaching organization that offers Master's and Ph.D. programs for the Study of Leadership and Change.

For more information about these and other programs, please visit www.adizes.com.